EATING

MY

FEELINGS

EATING

MY

FEELINGS

Tales of Overeating,

Underperforming, and Coping with

My Crazy Family

Mark Brennan Rosenberg

THREE RIVERS PRESS
NEW YORK

Published in the United States by Three Rivers Press,
an imprint of the Crown Publishing Group, a division of
Random House, Inc., New York.
www.crownpublishing.com

Three Rivers Press and the Tugboat design are registered
trademarks of Random House, Inc.

Library of Congress Cataloging-in-Publication Data
Rosenberg, Mark (Mark Brennan)
Eating my feelings / Mark Rosenberg
1. Rosenberg, Mark (Mark Brennan) 2. Comedians–
United States–Biography. 3. Weight loss–Humor. 4. Body
image–Humor. I. Title.
PN2287.R7576A3 2013
818'.603–dc23
[B]
2012045470

ISBN 978-0-385-34780-8
eISBN 978-0-385-34781-5

Printed in the United States of America

Book design by Maria Elias
Cover design by Kyle Kolker
Cover photographs: (ice cream cone) Michael Valdez/
iStock; (sprinkles on ice cream) Tetra Images/Superstock;
(sunglasses) Jonathan Downey/iStock;
(sprinkles on back) Mayakova/shutterstock
Author photograph: Eric Pietrangolare

10 9 8 7 6 5 4 3 2 1

First Edition

For Jason.
Every day you are missed.
In loving memory.

CONTENTS

Just Call Me Oprah
1

Homey Most Certainly Don't Play That
5

Choose Your Own Religion
16

The Great Birthday Cake Fiasco
33

Heavyweights
41

The Fifty-Dollar Diet
83

Blow-Job Betty
98

Sexy Pants
111

As the Revolving Door of Delivery Men Turns
123

All Shook Up
132

The Flyer Boy Follies
140

Tuesdays with Ricky
152

The Joy of Sex
164

The P90X-Files
171

Searching for Jackie Collins
221

Family Affair
228

Acknowledgments
241

EATING

MY

FEELINGS

JUST CALL ME OPRAH

I've had more ups and downs with my weight than Oprah. Unlike Oprah, however, no one really gives a shit. I've never carted all of my fat onto a soundstage in a wheelbarrow. There have been no cameras following me around while I hike my fat, black ass up forty flights of stairs. I've had my issues with food, but America was not watching, until now.

I guess I should introduce myself. My name is Mark Brennan Rosenberg and I'm pretty much a whiter, skinnier, gayer version of Oprah with a much filthier dialect. True, I don't have my own talk show or my OWN Network, but the similarities between the two of us are unbounded. Oprah has struggled with her weight and so have I. Oprah has spent hundreds of thousands of dollars on diets, trainers, and nutritionists and so have I. Oprah is a strong black woman and so am I. Unlike Oprah, I go even further, dig deeper, and get to the underbelly of how bad weight issues can get. I've never seen an episode of *Oprah* that tackled the nightmare of eating birthday cake off the floor. Never have I seen an episode of her show that delves into what can happen when you want to fuck your personal trainer, but have absolutely no intention of actually working out. I'm also quite certain that Oprah doesn't have Grindr on her iPhone. Well, guess what? I do. I am picking up where she left off and we are leaving no stone unturned and no bucket of chicken uneaten.

Together, you and I are going to take a journey into my struggles with weight, food, and body image. I know if you're reading this that means you're on page two. I know, books are long and reading is very hard and God forbid you create a world within your own imagination when you could be watching *Jersey Shore*. If you picked up this book and actually bought it, you probably only did so because you liked the cover, you are a friend of mine, or I verbally threatened you to do so, but have no fear. What you are about to read is a series of essays, all of which have a recurring theme. Meaning you can read one, a few, or all of them without hurting yourself from thinking too hard. I find this helpful to know beforehand, as most people these days seem to have the attention spans of guinea pigs.

Before we begin this magical voyage, here are some definitions of a few phrases that are mentioned throughout the book, just so you know what they mean ahead of time.

- **"Swamp Ass"**: Swamp ass happens when you go from cold to hot or hot to cold and your ass sweats so much that your underwear sticks to it.

- **"Body Be Right"**: This is a common phrase I like to say when I see a guy with a really killer body. Its meaning is heightened when you say it with the inflection that a fourteen-year-old black girl may use.

- **"Date-Rape-Drug Wasted"**: This commonly happens at gay bars when a guy is so drunk that you think he could potentially have been date-rape drugged.

- **"Eating My Feelings"**: Well . . . we'll get to that one in due time.

It may also be helpful to know some of the pop-culture references I refer to as well. I'm a child of the 1980s and '90s, and since no one has an appreciation for the classics anymore, it may help to briefly discuss a few things I reference frequently.

- *Clueless:* A movie that came out in the 1990s that propelled Alicia Silverstone to superstardom for about six months and gave America catchphrases like "as if." If you don't know what this movie is, then you probably aren't (A) gay or (B) a girl who grew up in the 1990s. If you don't fall into one of those categories, you should probably stop reading this book right now.

- *All My Children:* A daytime television show that introduced the world to Erica Kane, the woman America loves to hate. In fact, my first book, *Blackouts and Breakdowns* (currently on sale in bookstores everywhere), was dedicated to her.

- *Dynasty:* A very popular 1980s nighttime drama that featured women in dresses with shoulder pads fighting in lily ponds over a man who was in his late seventies and probably couldn't get it up anyway. Also known as the greatest show in television history.

Now that we've covered that, get ready for a shit parade beyond your wildest dreams. If you're hesitant about reading on, just pretend that Oprah actually wrote this book. I'm pretty sure she would approve.

HOMEY MOST CERTAINLY

DON'T PLAY THAT

Our story begins in a sleepy suburban town outside of Washington, D.C. Our heroine, Mark, an overweight ten-year-old with an affinity for soap operas and show tunes, has found himself in a delicate condition that raises the questions: How much Halloween candy is too much? How inadvertently racist, offensive, and foulmouthed can one boy be at such a tender age? How did he get that way?

Y ou can do what you wanna do . . . in living color."
    Every Sunday night I parked my fat ten-year-old ass on the couch to watch the most glorious television show ever, *In Living Color*. For whatever reason, I thought it was the funniest program on TV, but my parents thought otherwise.
    "Mark, I don't think that program is suitable for someone as

young as you," my mother would say. My mother is how I imagine all middle-aged housewives to be. Very well put together on the outside, bat-shit crazy on the inside. She basically embodies all of the characteristics of a person I would call a friend in adulthood, which is why we're besties now.

"But, Mom," I would retort, "they have the Fly Girls."

I always wanted to be a Fly Girl. In my opinion, that was about as high on the entertainment food chain as you could get.

Not only did *In Living Color* have Fly Girls, it had pretty much everything you could want from a television show at the time. MC Lyte would make an occasional cameo, you could find out what was playing in theaters that week because the Men in Film would snap for the movies they liked, and there was of course the pièce de résistance: Homey D. Clown. I loved Homey—the ex-con who plays a clown—and his take-no-prisoners attitude toward life. If someone pissed him off, he would lash out by hitting them over the head with a sock full of tennis balls. Because Homey did not play that, many people were injured as he tried to delight the world. I know one ten-year-old he entertained, and that was me. I wanted to be Homey, except for that pesky ex-con part, because I had no desire to go to jail. For whatever reason, I always wanted to get back at "The Man," and although I had no idea who the man was, I knew I hated him because Homey had told me to. Perhaps it had something to do with that fact that I was a constantly hungry ten-year-old, filled with angst because my parents continued to refuse to serve cake for breakfast.

The fall of 1990 was magical. The world was delighting in the musical stylings of Taylor Dayne, and talented people such as Ian Ziering and Arsenio Hall were about to come into their own. I was wrapped up in third-grade bullshit and loving every minute of it. My best friend at the time, Kelly Harmon, had decided to rename herself yet again. She was now going to call herself "Katie." The previous year she had gone by Katherine. This confused me so I decided I would call her "Katie-Kelly-Katherine" in order to prevent any further confusion on my part. When Halloween rolled around, she told me that she was going to be Sleeping Beauty and asked me what I was going to be.

"I don't know," I replied. "I guess I'll be a hobo again."

For the last three years, I rocked out a fabulous hobo costume that my mother had designed. This may have something to do with the fact that most upper-middle-class families have never actually seen a homeless person; they do, however, seem to think hobo costumes are the most adorable outfit choice for children come Halloween.

"That's cool," Katie-Kelly-Katherine responded.

"Yeah," I replied, "but I have been a hobo like three times now and I am beginning to feel like making fun of homeless people is wrong." Bust out your soapbox, young Mark Rosenberg. "I don't have any ideas."

"You could go as Barney Rubble. Just turn your hobo gear into a brown frock and call it a day."

"Barney Rubble? What a dumbass idea," I replied, duly noted, and used the following Halloween. But this year I needed something with a little kick. Besides Katie-Kelly-Katherine, I had no other friends, and I wasn't quite sure how to make them. I was fat and the rest of the kids liked to play sports, not watch soap operas, so there was a definite divide in the friends department. On one side there was myself, a soap-opera-loving, brownie-baking tyke who appreciated everything Susan Lucci wore and had a strong affinity for things that glittered. On the other side there was everyone else. Luckily, I had a friend in Katie-Kelly-Katherine because she watched *All My Children* and the conversations were endless. The rest of the kids weren't as cool, and I think some of them watched NBC soaps, which was unacceptable as far as I was concerned, because if a soap opera didn't feature Erica Kane, Viki Buchanan, or Lucy Coe, there was no sense in watching it to begin with.

I needed to find a Halloween costume that would wow the class and get me as much candy as possible, but I had no idea where to find inspiration. I thought about going as Lucy Coe from *General Hospital* and wearing a hot red wedding dress, but quickly realized that would only be a good idea if I wanted to get punched in the neck repeatedly by every bully at school for the next fortnight. The Sunday before Halloween, I was sitting in front of the TV, and like a gift from Jesus Christ himself, I had the best idea ever.

"I KNOW!" I yelled. "I will go as Homey D. Clown for Halloween!"

"Who is Homey D. Clown?" my mother asked.

"He's the funny ex-con-turned-hilarious-clown on *In Living Color*," I said.

"I don't know," my mother said. "I'll sleep on it and get back to you."

The next day after school, we were off to Spencer's Gifts to buy my new kick-ass Halloween costume. We bought a huge red Afro wig, makeup, and an outfit just like Homey's. I was ecstatic that my mother was finally doing what I told her to do and thought it would be a nice segue into getting everything I wanted for Christmas. The next night was Halloween and fat kids everywhere were rejoicing, myself included. Halloween is the only holiday (aside from Thanksgiving and Kwanzaa, depending on your religious beliefs) when every child acts like a complete fat-ass. Every Halloween I regaled in the fact that yet again I would be able to eat as much candy as I wanted to, without being judged by my bone-thin brothers for gorging like a pig.

That evening, I put on my costume and filled a sock with tennis balls, just like Homey's. Red Afro wig: check. Yellow clown suit with big red buttons: check. Big floppy red shoes: double check. However, a very important aspect of the costume was missing. I just looked like a dumb-ass clown and it really wasn't the look I was going for. I was pissed.

"MOM!" I yelled.

"What the fuck are you yelling about?" she replied. That Halloween, all of the adults were coming over to my parents' house to get shit-faced while their kids went trick-or-treating. God bless the suburbs.

"I don't look like Homey at all," I said.

"Awww . . . you look cute," one of my mom's dumb drunk friends said.

"Seriously?" I replied. "I look like any dumb-ass, run-of-the-mill clown."

"Mark! Language!" my mother said.

The adults all laughed as I turned around and walked up the stairs. I felt defeated. I thought I had the most amazing costume idea ever, but now I was regretting my brilliant plan. I wandered into my parents' room to see if my mother had a red wedding dress lying around, thinking I could pull off Lucy Coe after all. After searching her closets for a hot second, I stumbled upon something of my father's and came up with an even better idea.

The doorbell rang and my mother answered: "Hello, dear."

"Hi, Mrs. Rosenberg," Katie-Kelly-Katherine responded.

"Hi, ah, Carrie?"

"It's Katie now."

"Right," my mother replied. "MAAAAARK! KATHY'S HEEEEERE!" She went back into the kitchen while Katie-Kelly-Katherine waited in the foyer. My house on Silverstone Court was amazing. We had a staircase that wrapped around the foyer, so every time I walked down it I pretended to be Krystle Carrington on the opening credits of *Dynasty*. Every morning, I would stroll down the stairs, stopping midway to pause, look at the camera that wasn't there, and continue walking. I loved her and her shoulder pads. I wanted to be her and I was every time I would strut down that spiral staircase. But that evening, I had a surprise that may have been better than Krystle Carrington herself bursting through our front door with news that Denver Carrington had been taken over once again by Alexis. I officially had the best Halloween costume ever.

"Katie-Kelly-Katherine, what's up?" I said as I breezed down the stairs.

"Mark," she replied, "what's all over your face?"

"Shoe polish," I said as I made my way down the stairs and greeted Katie-Kelly-Katherine in the foyer. "Now I really look like Homey D. Clown!"

I had taken my father's black shoe polish and smeared it all over my face. I thought, at age ten, that my Homey D. Clown costume would not be complete unless I was in blackface. In my mind, making fun of homeless people was a bad idea, but going out of doors as a satirical African American clown was completely acceptable.

"I suppose you do," Katie-Kelly-Katherine said.

"Thanks. Pretty amazing, huh?"

"I guess so," she said. "My mom doesn't let me watch *In Living Color,* though. She doesn't like the racial undertones. Whatever that means."

"Not sure. Let's get out of here."

It was the best Halloween ever. Katie-Kelly-Katherine and I hit up all of the rich people's houses and made out like bandits. Fortunately for me, my parading around the neighborhood in blackface didn't have anyone batting an eye because we hadn't yet come across a family of any color other than white. We wandered around all night collecting candy from everyone and our costumes were a hit. Katie-Kelly-Katherine totally looked like Sleeping Beauty and I, of course, looked exactly like Homey D. Clown. As we made our way back to Silverstone Court, we decided to hit up my neighbors for some last-minute treats. First we went to the Bauers' house. They lived directly across the street from us. I think Mrs. Bauer was kind of a lush, but being in an upper-middle-class neighborhood, everyone called her "eccentric."

"Oh hey," Mrs. Bauer said as she opened the door to her home.

"Trick or treat!" Katie-Kelly-Katherine and I said in harmony.

"Look at you kids," Mrs. Bauer said as the contents of her martini glass swished this way and that. "Candy? Is that you?"

"It's Katie!"

"Well, you look just like Sleeping Beauty," Mrs. Bauer said. "And who are you, young man?"

"It's me, Mrs. Bauer. Mark Rosenberg," I replied.

"Mark? What a costume! I barely recognized you," Mrs. Bauer said. "You Rosenbergs. You're Catholic. You're Jewish. And apparently today, you're black. Good luck with that," she said as she dumped candy into our pillowcases and slammed the door.

I wondered if she was hammered or just high on prescription pills as we made our way to their next-door neighbors, the Phillipses. They had a deaf son named Jeff, who we all hated. We may have hated him because he was deaf (kids can be so cruel), but he had a really bad attitude. Earlier in the year, being the fat, gay, equally-as-hated ten-year-old, I decided I was going to try and reach out to Jeff by learning sign language, which apparently pissed him off further. He was so mean to everyone; it's no wonder he was home when we knocked on the Phillipses' door for candy.

"Karen? Is that you?" Jeff said.

"It's Katie!"

"Trick or treat, Jeff," I said.

"We're out of candy," Jeff said.

"I couldn't fully understand you because of your little 'problem,'" Katie-Kelly-Katherine said, referring to the fact that Jeff was deaf, making it harder for us to understand him. "Are you trying to tell me that you're out of candy?"

"Yeah. Seriously."

"You're such an asshole, Jeff," I said.

"You're just calling me an asshole because I'm deaf, aren't you?"

"No, Jeff," I responded. "I'm calling you an asshole because you're an asshole. And my father is still pissed that your parents put up that sign that says Caution: Deaf Child, right in front of our mailbox."

"You two suck! Get off of my property! And while you're at it, wash that crap off your face, Mark. I may be deaf, but you look like a fool!" Jeff said as he slammed the door in our faces.

"God, I hate that kid," I replied. He was almost as bad as that fucking Russian family that lived down the street who continued to refuse to take part in our American tradition of celebrating Halloween. We knew they were home; they just wouldn't answer the door when we knocked. We then walked to the house directly next to ours, the Goodmans.

The Goodmans were like the Huxtables from *The Cosby Show*. The father was a doctor, the mother was just plain fabulous, and they were the only black family within a three-mile radius. I really liked Mike, their son, but he went to private school because they were cooler than us. Katie-Kelly-Katherine and I rolled up to their home and knocked on the door. Dr. Goodman answered.

"What. The. Fuck?" Dr. Goodman said.

"Trick or treat," we said in unison.

"What the fuck is this?" Dr. Goodman asked.

"I'm Sleeping Beauty," Katie-Kelly-Katherine said.

"And I'm Homey D. Clown," I said. "Homey D. Clown. Homey D. Clown. Don't mess around. Don't mess around!" I sang.

"Nice costume, Cassie," Dr. Goodman said.

"IT'S KATIE!"

"Mark, your costume is . . . interesting. Do your parents know you have been walking around in blackface?"

"Ummm . . . I actually can't be sure," I replied.

"Interesting. I am going to have to have a little talk with them," Dr. Goodman said. "You know, that's very racist."

"I just didn't want to be a hobo again," I cried. My plight for the homeless continued: "I just feel so bad for them. I mean, they have nowhere to live. Essentially, they are home*less*. Without a home. Hence why they are called homeless people."

"Yes, I understand, being homeless is a bad thing," Dr. Goodman said. "Come inside." Katie-Kelly-Katherine and I entered the Goodman home and Dr. Goodman gave us a forty-five-minute rundown of the tribulations of the African American and why blackface was racist. We did however get to enjoy a few musical numbers from *The Jazz Singer,* so it was not only educational, but entertaining as well. Just like a killer episode of *Reading Rainbow.*

I went home and washed the shoe polish off my face. I began counting the treats that I had acquired that evening. I always counted and categorized my Halloween candy so that my brothers wouldn't get their grubby little hands on it. As I was sorting, my mother came into my room in a panic.

"MARK! DON'T EAT THAT CANDY!" she yelled.

"What the hell?" I said.

"There is a rapist or a serial killer or a child molester or something on the loose and he's poisoned bags of candy," my mother said. This was coming from a woman who believed pretty much anything she was told. Earlier that year, she was convinced that Bat Boy had given birth outside of the National Cathedral, so all of her children were told to steer clear. She was also an advertiser's dream come true. If JoBeth Williams told my mother to buy Playtex, you better believe she bought it.

"Are you hammered right now?"

"No." She paused. "Well...a little. But it's true! Now give me your candy before you're poisoned too," she said as she gathered all of the candy that I had just categorized on my bed and dumped it into the trash can. Knowing I was not above eating out of a trash can, she took the can and dumped it into the garbage outside.

"DAMN THAT WOMAN!" I yelled. She had taken my

candy away, and with it she took my childhood as well. All I wanted to do was acquire as much candy as possible so I could gorge like a pig and not get judged for being a fat-ass, and now my mother had totally ruined my plan.

Because of this experience, I learned never to judge people by the color of their skin, what they look like, or where they are from, even when I was trying to use it to my advantage to get free food. I hate everyone regardless of any of that.

CHOOSE YOUR OWN RELIGION

Every good story needs a good villain, and Mark found his in his evil whore of a stepmother, Stacey. Our heroine's father is about to drop the biggest bombshell of all time on Mark and his beloved siblings. As our journey through Mark's fatness continues, he finds the answer to the question philosophers have been plagued with for years: What's so fucking great about being Jewish anyway?

There is always a lot of confusion as to who belongs to what religion in my family. So let's clear a few things up: My mother is Catholic. When she had her first child—my oldest brother, Tony—he was baptized and raised Catholic. While all of this was going down, my father—who is a Jew—was married to his first wife, a lovely woman named Faith. They had two daughters—twins, my sisters Kimmy and Jamie—and raised them Jewish. Then my father married my mother and adopted my oldest brother, Tony, because his father had apparently been abducted by aliens and left my mother shortly after Tony was born. Then my parents got together and had me and my little brother, Kevin. So the Rosenberg clan is essentially the quintessential American family with a mixture of different religions, beliefs, and levels of guilt. When you mix Irish Catholic and Jewish, you have one drunk, guilty household on your hands.

When I was very little, my parents' religious differences never interfered with everyday life. Kevin and I were both baptized and went to Catholic school and my father never seemed to mind. To appease my father our family even celebrated the important Jewish holidays, so he could teach his children about his own beliefs. All was quiet on the religious front. That is until my parents got a divorce and my father decided to remarry a Jewish whore named Stacey.

Stacey was more like a high-class escort with a law degree and less of a whore, but I hated her nonetheless and my hatred for her began early on. She was, in my eyes, evil in its purest form. She had the air of Cruela De Vil every time she walked in the room, except she had an even worse hairdo. I'm also pretty sure she had murdered a puppy or two before meeting my father. I believe that I hated Stacey so early on because my mother had this unwarranted assumption that she and my father had had an affair before he divorced my mother. With no evidence to prove her story as truth, I took my mother's side without any question of whether she was right or not, as anyone would do. Shortly after Stacey and my father began dating, they got married and didn't tell anyone. That is, until the day of my elementary school graduation. All five of my father's children and Stacey's son, Paco (who shared with me a mutual love of Julie Andrews films and cake. I liked him and would have considered

him an ally if his mother hadn't danced on the devil's play-
ground), gathered at our favorite Chinese restaurant for what
we thought was a casual evening of moo shu and shooting the
shit, until my father dropped the biggest bombshell ever.

"We have news," my father said as he bit into an eggroll.

"Your father and I got married," Stacey said as she showed
off the huge ring my father had given her.

"Is this a joke? I said. "Are we being filmed for *Candid Camera* or something?" Where was Dom DeLuise when I needed
him most?

"Nope, when we were on vacation in Orlando last weekend,
your father and I decided to tie the knot. We brought pictures!"
Stacey said as she began passing around photos of "the big day."
I sat there in disbelief. At the tender age of eleven, I could not
picture my father with anyone other than my mother, even
though they had tried to kill each other at least five times each.
No eleven-year-old wants to see his father married to someone
other than his mother, especially not if that certain someone is
the whore of Babylon. I also didn't want him to be with a woman
who was so emotionally unhinged that a blind man could sense
her craziness at twenty paces. "Well, I certainly have lost all desire to visit the state of Florida ever again," my sister Jamie said
as she passed the wedding photos to my brother Tony.

"I don't get it," my little brother Kevin said. "What about
Mom?"

"Your mother will move on," Stacey said. "Or you can call
me Mom now, if you want to."

"I am not going to be able to get the taste of vomit out of
my mouth for the rest of the day. Thanks, Stacey," my sister
Kimmy said.

"Kimberly!" my father barked. "Please try to treat your new

stepmother with a little respect." Had Stacey done anything to garner any ounce of respect, perhaps she would have.

While looking at the wedding pictures, Tony said that they needed to change the city's name from Orlando to Whorlando now that Stacey had visited. My father quickly realized that news of his wedding was not getting the warm reception he had hoped. I could see defeat in his eyes. All he really wanted was to move on from my mother, but everyone else at the table knew that the person he had chosen to move on with was evil in its purest form. Tony handed the wedding pictures to me and I glanced through them. I quickly stumbled upon a picture of Stacey's son, Paco, hugging Mickey Mouse.

"Wait . . . what?" I gasped. "Why is Paco hugging Mickey Mouse? Did you all get married and stop at Disney World on your way home?"

"It's not what it looks like," my father replied.

"You've got to be fucking kidding me with this right now," I replied. I had been pushing for a trip to Disney World for the last eighteen months.

"We needed a witness for the wedding," Stacey replied.

"Seriously, bitch? Don't play me like that," I said.

"Are you calling my mother a bitch?" Paco asked as he got up from his seat in anger. I quickly shut my mouth before getting my ass kicked.

"So wait a second, you took Paco on vacation, told none of us about it, then decided to get married?" Jamie said. "This is bullshit."

"It's not what it looks like," my father replied. "We needed a witness."

"I've been to Florida plenty of times," Kim said. "Give a Cuban a few bucks and there's your witness."

"We wanted it to be special," Stacey said.

"Wait a second," Tony said as he looked at his watch. "I have about three weeks left to deal with all of you in person before I go off to college and decide whether or not I pick up the phone when you call," he said. "And I drove here, so I don't need to sit through this."

Tony grabbed Kimmy and Jamie and left Kevin and me to fend for ourselves at the Chinese restaurant with my father, the whore-bag, and Paco. The waitress came by our table to refill our water, but quickly fled as she saw my older brother and sisters leave the restaurant in a frenzy. I don't know if I was more pissed that my father, Stacey, and Paco had taken a trip to Disney World without me or that my father had married quite possibly the most evil person in the world and opted not to let any of his children in on it until the day of *my* elementary school graduation, the most important day of a young man's life. Saying I was pissed was an understatement. For the first time in my life, I had lost my appetite. I had a plateful of chicken-fried rice sitting in front of me and I couldn't eat. Stacey's marriage to my father had made me anorexic. Well, at least for the rest of the evening.

My father drove my little brother and me to my elementary school graduation, where my mother was waiting for us. Before accepting my diploma, I told my mother I had some serious gossip for her after the ceremony. As I walked onto the stage, I heard her yelling: "WHAT THE FUCK?" I realized that there was no need for hair braiding, cookies, and gossip afterward because she had already found out the news.

Little did I know my elementary school graduation was not going to be the only important day ruined by my arch nemesis. She went out of her way to ruin everything for me, and my father allowed her to do it. A few years into their marriage, the big question of "Who is going to die Jewish?" came into play. I believed that my father wanted to pressure Kevin and me into becoming Jewish to stick it to my mother one last time.

When I was around twelve years old, Stacey broached the subject for the first time.

"How would you like to have a Bar Mitzvah?" she asked.

"How would you like to go fuck yourself?" I replied.

"MARK!" my father yelled. "Watch your language and listen to what your stepmother is asking you."

"It would be fun," Stacey said. "You can have a big party and get lots of gifts," she continued, "and if you do a good job, you can take a trip anywhere you want to go. I hear Disney World is lovely this time of year."

"Seriously?" I asked. I knew what they were doing. At this point, they both should have known where my loyalties lay. I was on Team Trish and nothing was going to sway my vote. I knew if I had a Bar Mitzvah, it would crush my mother, and that was exactly why my stepmother had proposed this idea in the first place.

"You're both retarded," I replied. "I know your game, woman," I said to Stacey, "and I ain't playin' it!" The only reason I even spoke to my father or stepmother was because I was court ordered to. I literally *had* to see them every other weekend and once a week. That period in my father's life was miserable for everyone involved. I hated Stacey, if not for conversations like this one, then for the fact that she was a straight-up cunt.

I could see panic in my father's eyes. He wanted so badly for his younger boys to be Jewish to impress his new wife and knew his window of opportunity was closing. I was already thirteen, was a borderline racist, and had a mouth like a sailor that could preclude me from ever setting foot in any temple. Watching *One Life to Live* every day allowed me to spot a crook from a mile away. I knew Stacey's trickery and certainly wasn't dumb enough to fall for it. So my father focused on my little brother, Kevin. He was always an easier target because he was younger and did not watch as much television as I did.

Shortly after our conversation, Kevin came back to my mother with exciting news: "I am going to have a Bar Mitzvah!"

I think my mother may have done a spit-take in response to this, but regained her composure with, "Okay, Kevin, whatever you want to do."

I sat there wishing I had been able to shield my little brother from my evil stepmother's clutches, but knew it was too late.

"Stacey said that I could have a big party and take a trip wherever I wanted to go. It's going to be so much fun," Kevin replied. Little did he know about the three years of rigorous work he was going to have to put in before having this big party and taking this wonderful trip. Kids are so stupid. Shortly after Kevin left the room, my mother picked up the phone and called my father.

"WHAT THE FUCK IS THIS ABOUT KEVIN HAVING A BAR MITZVAH?" she yelled into the phone.

"It's his decision," my father said.

I know what you're thinking. How did I know what my father was saying on the other end of the phone? Two words: Erica Kane. She taught me everything I needed to know about the art of eavesdropping, so naturally, I was listening in on the other phone with my finger on the mute button.

"He told me that you and"—she stopped herself—"I can't bear to say her name, but that woman, promised him a big party and a big trip. Is that true?"

"Of course not. I mean he would obviously have a big party. That's what a Bar Mitzvah is."

"No it isn't, you idiot!" my mother said. "You don't even know your own fucking religion. Having a Bar Mitzvah is not just a huge party. Thank God my father is not alive, because he would kill you right now."

"Calm down, Pat."

"You know that if my father were alive right now, none of this would be happening. But I will not get in the way of what is going to make Kevin happy, and since you've already put it in his head that he's going to do this, I guess I can't fight it or I'll be the bad guy."

"He has made his mind up and we should just let him do what he wants to do," my father said.

"No, you and that bitch made his mind up. I cannot believe that you are doing any of this, but I will tell you one thing right now. I am not paying for any of this shit. You and that slut can take care of it and don't forget to invite my side of the family. You know they like to party." With that, my mother hung up the phone.

My father had won this round, and my mother knew it. She looked at me after I rejoined her from the other room and asked, "Why aren't you having a Bar Mitzvah?"

I didn't want to tell her it was because I would forever remain on her team, so instead replied, "It's too much work. That and I hate Stacey, so I try to do the opposite of what would make her happy."

The news of Kevin's impending Bar Mitzvah spread like wildfire on my mother's side of the family—mainly because I have a big mouth. My cousins and I all stood as a united front to poke jabs at Kevin whenever we got the chance. Now, not only did we have his big head to make fun of, we had his Judaism as well. When the holidays rolled around, I became particularly irritated.

"I don't understand why Kevin continues to get Christmas presents when he is clearly a Jew now!" I said to my mother.

"Because I celebrate Christmas and if your brother is with me for the holidays, then he will get presents."

"This is bullshit!" I replied. "I don't get to have a big party or take a trip, but Kevin gets whatever he wants from both parents. It's not fair!"

"Life isn't fair, Mark," my mother told me, as if by now I hadn't already gotten the memo on that one.

"My loyalty to you obviously means nothing," I said.

"What the hell are you talking about?"

After realizing my mother didn't know that the only reason I had decided not to have a Bar Mitzvah was because I wanted to remain loyal to her, I quickly retreated to my room.

However, I never stopped talking about how big of a Jew Kevin was and how it wasn't fair that he got to celebrate every single holiday. Easter in particular pissed me off.

"So, let me get this straight," I said to my brother. "You don't even believe that Jesus Christ is our Lord and Savior, so why the hell are you celebrating his resurrection from the dead?"

"Because Mom is making me go to church, Mark," Kevin replied. I simply did not understand why this Jew was even allowed in a church. Granted, he wasn't a real Jew yet, but he obviously wasn't Catholic anymore. He just wanted a party and a trip. In my opinion, Kevin should have been barred from all religions for being a dumb-ass. One Easter Sunday, my mother, brother, and I all sat in church and listened to the sermon. Quite frankly, I believe a good back-from-the-dead story line is best saved for daytime television, but I can buy into it once a year on Easter. I don't think Kevin was really listening, because he was a big Jew now, but all I could do was wonder why he was there in the first place. He'd picked a religion, but was spoiling in the riches of another because apparently the Easter Bunny breezed into Jewish kids' homes now as well. As we were all getting ready to leave, the priest was sprinkling holy water on the congregation as they were exiting. When my mother, Kevin, and I were about to leave and I saw the priest raise the water to sprinkle Kevin, I did a slow-motion death grab and jumped in his way.

"Mark! What the hell are you doing?" my mother asked.

"Shielding the Jew from the holy water," I replied.

"Jew?" the priest asked.

"Don't worry about it," my mother said as she hustled us out of the church as fast as she possibly could. "Mark, you are so embarrassing."

"What's more embarrassing, me blocking Kevin from the holy water or Kevin being a Jew?"

She didn't answer. That was the last time I ever went to that particular church, because my mother had never been more embarrassed in her life. I decided it was time to put on my Nancy Drew hat and do a little digging to see what it was exactly that was going on at this mystical place they called a synagogue.

A few days after Easter, I took the bus to the local temple to see if all the brouhaha about being Jewish was worth dividing our family over. Because lines had been drawn in the sand, mainly by my big mouth, I felt confused about why I was so against Kevin having a Bar Mitzvah in the first place. I knew I did not want to appease Stacey, but perhaps I was a bit out of line in judging Kevin's decision. After riding the bus with several of our community's finest toothless old ladies, I arrived at the temple ready to get to the bottom of my big Jewish question.

I suddenly felt like a real-life Nancy Drew. But instead of solving the case of who killed the man at the old mill, I was cracking the case of why the Jews were the chosen people. Had I been about fifty pounds lighter, an actual girl, and on a mission that had some sort of purpose other than sticking it to my stepmother, I really could have been Nancy Drew. I had every intention of lying to the rabbi and telling him that I was going to convert so I could get insider secrets to help me figure out why all of this religion business meant so much to everyone in my family.

"Can I help you, young man?" said a lovely white-haired woman as I entered.

"Yes," I replied. "I would like to speak to someone about converting."

She looked me up and down and smiled. "Of course, young man. Take a seat and I will see if there is a rabbi around to speak with you."

The elderly woman walked down a long hallway and into a room, then shut the door behind her. As I sat and waited for someone to come out and speak with me, I looked around the temple. Gone were the crucifixes, prayer candles, and Stations of the Cross that made my church such a welcoming place. Instead there were beautiful stained-glass windows in a room that simply had a podium with a large case behind it. This placed rocked! I had already concluded that the case was filled with candies and cakes to eat every Friday night after temple ended. In my imagination, temple had one-upped church in every way imaginable. Apparently, Kevin had it right all along. Blinded by my imagination of the wonders of what this place held, I then turned my attention back to the hallway to see the woman walking back in my direction with a short man behind her.

"Young man, this is Rabbi Silverman," the woman said to me.

"I think this place is great," I said as I stood to shake the rabbi's hand. "Really like what you've done with it."

The rabbi smiled as the older woman left us. He sat down next to me.

"What can I help you with?" the rabbi asked.

"Well," I said as I cleared my throat. I had quickly learned as a child of the Catholic Church not to fuck with a figurehead, so I put my big-boy hat on for this conversation. "I'm thinking about converting."

"Do your parents know where you are right now?" he asked.

"Ummm . . . yeah," I said.

The rabbi knew I was lying.

"No, they don't," I replied. "I lied to you. I'm going to hell now, aren't I?"

"Our people don't believe in hell," the rabbi said.

"HOLY CRAP! JEWS REALLY DO ROCK!" I yelled. "No hell! This is awesome!" Having been told several times that week alone that I was going to hell, this was a huge relief. I already understood why Kevin had chosen Judaism over Catholicism. Not only was the decor a lot more welcoming, there was no hell, and a cabinet full of treats were ready for me to devour after the pizza party I had decided was included after temple concluded on Friday nights.

"That doesn't mean you can run around doing whatever you'd like," the rabbi said, smiling. "What is it exactly that I can do for you?"

"Well," I said, "my younger brother, Kevin, has decided to convert to Judaism and I was wondering if I should as well."

"I'm sorry," the rabbi began, "your younger brother? How old are you? Twelve? Why are so many people in your family converting to different religions?"

After giving the rabbi what would have been an epic Power-Point presentation on my family, its lineage, and religious background, the rabbi scratched his head and responded: "You have a very interesting family," he said. "What do you believe in?"

I had to think about this. I had been persuaded by so many people to believe in so many different things at this point, I wasn't quite sure what I actually believed in.

"I believe I love my mom and dad and brothers and sisters," I said. "I believe in God, but I'm not sure where he is and I'm not one hundred percent sure that whole 'back-from-the-dead' nonsense would hold up in a court of law. I believe that I sometimes say mean things, but I am a good person and I believe that the people will forgive me for the mean things I say."

"Then that's all you need to believe in for now," the rabbi said. "You're still a child, and I think you may be a bit confused because of what is going on with your family. You follow your path, and if it leads you back here, we will welcome you with open arms."

"Thanks, man," I replied, "but let's say I wanted to convert. What would I have to do?"

"Well, first you'd have to learn Hebrew—" he began to say.

I stopped him. "You've already lost me. I would need to learn a new language?" I asked. I barely had a handle on English at this point, and there was no way in hell I would be able to throw a second form of communication into the mix. "No dice!"

The rabbi smiled as we both got up and began walking toward the door.

"You're welcome back whenever you like," Rabbi Silverman said.

"Yeah, I know, my last name is Rosenberg. I kind of figured I could come and go as I pleased."

I got back on the bus and once home, made a beeline straight for my brother's room.

"KEVIN!" I yelled as I flung open the door to his room.

"What do you want?" he asked. He must have been pretty exhausted by my constant badgering him about his shift in religion.

"I just got back from temple," I said.

"I thought you went to the store to get brownie mix," Kevin said.

"I lied." It was so effortless for me at age twelve; I didn't even bother apologizing for it anymore.

"Why were you at temple?" Kevin asked.

"Because I wanted to see what all the fuss was about," I said. "Seems pretty cool to me. I am dying to know what is in the cabinets at the front of the room. Do you think it's cookies?"

"No, you moron! That's where they keep the Torah."

"Oh." My sudden interest in Judaism was waning. "Anyway, I want to know why you want to become a Jew so badly." I had to case the joint myself, but wanted to hear it straight from the horse's mouth. "Is it because you want a party? Or are you just trying to get in good with Stacey? I don't trust her, she's got shifty eyes."

"This has nothing to do with Stacey," Kevin said. "I've thought a lot about this. I really want to become a Jew because it's what I believe in."

"But what about all of the church we went to and the religion shoved down our throats for all of these years?"

"But it's not what I believe in. When you're Jewish you can question your religion. When you're Catholic, you must do what you're told and that's that. That's not what I want out of my religion."

Suddenly I realized that Kevin becoming a Jew was not the debacle I was making it out to be.

"Being a Jew sounds great," I said.

"Then why don't you become one too?" Kevin asked.

"I thought about it, but apparently you have to learn a whole new language and shit and quite frankly, I don't have the time for that." It was true. My afternoons were best spent watching daytime television, which is really the closest thing to a ritual I've ever had in my life. "But good luck," I told Kevin, "and Godspeed."

I left Kevin's room and felt good about his decision to continue on his journey to become a good Jew. My journey, on the other hand, led me to the couch with a bucket of chicken and reruns of *Petticoat Junction,* which was not nearly as rewarding but certainly a hell of a lot more entertaining.

Three years passed and it was finally time for Kevin's big day. Having experienced firsthand what a shit show Bar Mitzvahs could be thanks to my sisters' double Bat Mitzvah a few years back, I eagerly awaited what Kevin's would hold. After temple, where no cookies were served, we were all escorted to "Kevin's Diner." They had turned our local country club into a diner with Kevin's name as the theme. Everything was Kevin and nothing was Mark. Typical. I immediately let my brother know that I thought a diner theme was ridiculous and that he should have gone with a Mardi Gras theme, but he didn't care. He had a good time and he deserved it, despite my complaining. Even my mother was on board with the merriment. She had the time of her life, and why wouldn't she have? More than 75 percent of the guests that evening were her Irish Catholic family members, in what I was told was a first for such an occasion.

Now pushing sixteen, I, on the other hand, experienced a series of firsts that night. I drank my first White Russian, had my first one-hundred-dollar steak, and smoked my first cigarette. I still blame my brother for my addiction to cigarettes. That summer, Kevin got his big trip: a journey to the Holy Land. My father decided to take Kevin and Stacey to Israel and Africa as a present for becoming a Jew. Shortly after, I found out that Paco and his girlfriend were joining them as well.

"So wait, everyone is going on vacation, except me. Again?" I asked my father.

"You didn't want to have a Bar Mitzvah," my father replied.

"Paco is like twenty-two. And his girlfriend isn't even a part of this family. Why are they going and I'm not?"

"Stacey invited them."

"You do realize that you are missing my triumphant return to the stage this summer, in the dinner theater's epic production of *Bye Bye Birdie*?"

"See, you couldn't have gone on this trip anyway," my father said.

"I wouldn't do the show if I got to go to Israel and Africa, you moron."

"Don't call your father a moron," Stacey chimed in.

"I'm sorry, I meant to say idiot."

Stacey then proceeded to roll her eyes at me, which quickly turned into our only form of communication.

Everyone went on vacation but me, again. I stayed behind and sang "*A Lot of Livin' to Do*" four times a week at a dinner theater for old people eating sixteen-dollar steaks.

THE GREAT BIRTHDAY
CAKE FIASCO

Our heroine's fight against good and evil continued. As Mark's father and stepmother lived out every episode of *The Tom & Jerry Show* in real life, Mark was given even more hurdles to leap. Not only was Stacey hell-bent on forcing Mark to partake in outdoor activities, she was also forcing him to bake a birthday cake that would forever put a crack in the faulty foundation of their family.

When my father moved in with my new stepmother, they decided their first decision as a parental team would be to buy my little brother and me Rollerblades.

"But it's January," I said. "What the hell am I supposed to do with Rollerblades in January?"

"Why can't you just appreciate the fact that you're getting a present?" my father asked.

"Because, this present is ridiculous, number one. Number two: this is probably another lame attempt at getting me off the couch and out of doors. Not going to work."

"YOU WILL ROLLERBLADE!" my father yelled.

"Whatever. *Mary Poppins* is on Turner Classic Movies. That's what I will be doing this afternoon." Not that it made one bit of difference whether it was on TV or not, I owned two copies of the film. I just needed an excuse to stay inside.

It was around this point when my evil stepmother walked into the room. She was probably drinking whiskey on the rocks and saying nasty things about my mother under her breath.

"Those skates cost a fortune," the evil whore said. "Get your ass up and get outside NOW!"

"It's like thirty degrees out," I replied.

My stepmother grabbed the Rollerblades, threw them at me, and watched as I attempted to put them on.

"I CURSE THE DAY YOU WERE BOTH BORN!" I yelled.

"Speaking of which," my stepmother said, "tomorrow is your father's birthday. You boys should bake him a cake. I bought cake mix, so when you come in from Rollerblading, that can be your next activity for the day."

My father put his arm around my stepmother and they both smiled. I really hoped that they were not thinking, "Wow, we are really great parents," because they weren't. I would have been better off being raised by Mexican vultures.

Kevin and I put our Rollerblades on and went outside. It was freezing and our street was basically one huge hill that led to a busy intersection at the bottom. I began to think that my stepmother was trying to kill me. It had recently snowed so the street was very icy. Here I was, never having Rollerbladed in my life, standing outside on an icy hill and grossly overweight. Yes, I thought, my stepmother is trying to kill me.

Kevin, of course, had no problem learning how to Rollerblade. He was eight years old, raised as a Jew, played soccer, and was everything my father and moronic stepmother would want in a child—except for the fact that he really liked to set fires on occasion. Meanwhile, here I was, eleven years old, as gay as the day is May, and about fifty pounds overweight. There was no way I was going to be able to Rollerblade.

I took a step onto the street and immediately fell flat on my ass. What the hell was my father thinking leaving me out here to fend for myself? It was freezing and I was dressed like I was auditioning for the sequel to *A Christmas Story*. I got myself up, turned around, and tried to open the door to our house, but it was locked.

"You're not coming back in the house until you at least try to Rollerblade," my stepmother yelled from inside as she looked at the now-empty glass in her hand, thus prompting her to turn to the kitchen for a refill.

"You've got to be kidding me," I said under my breath. "What a whore."

I decided I would do what I did best: give it a half-assed attempt and begin complaining so much that my father would have no choice but to let me back into the house.

I got back up and began my second attempt at Rollerblading. I gathered my bearings and began to glide on the icy street. Suddenly I was headed straight down the hill toward the busy intersection at the end of our street.

"HOLY SHIT!" I yelled. I had no idea how to stop. I was

surely going to get hit by a car and meet an untimely death. All that was running through my head was that I hoped the newspaper article that reported on my horrific death read: "Child Dies Because Stepmother Is a Stupid Bitch."

My arms were up as if I were flying down the hill. I quickly realized that was probably making me go faster, so I abruptly dropped my hands to my sides. Cars were racing through the intersection at the bottom of the hill and I saw my life flash before my eyes. I remembered being a baby and how happy I was as a child. Then I laughed as I remembered my brother shitting his pants on the way to school one fall morning and my father being so frantic over it that he nearly totaled his car after hitting a tree. I then remembered my beloved mother and how she would always allow me to watch any Julie Andrews movie I wanted. Even that flop of an Alfred Hitchcock film she was in. I suddenly flashed back to reality. I wasn't going to let my stepmother win this round. She wasn't getting rid of me that easily. I knew what I had to do and knew it was going to result in a world of pain.

I sat down as if I was about to take a dump and landed flat on my ass.

"MOTHERFUCKER THAT HURT!" I yelled.

I got out of the middle of the street and crawled up the adjacent sidewalk that was covered in snow. God only knows where the hell my brother went at this point. Apparently, saving my life was not on his radar that day. He was probably inside drinking hot cocoa and laughing at what a fat-ass I was. I continued crawling up the hill until I reached our house.

I walked up the stairs. I had taken my skates off and was now standing on the ice in my socks. I tried to open the door but it was still locked. I looked inside to see my father, stepmother, and brother sitting on the couch watching *Mary Poppins.*

"Assholes," I said under my breath. I began ringing the doorbell.

My father ran to the door and opened it.

"What happened to you?" he asked.

"I almost died," I replied as I entered the house. I was dripping wet and had a huge stain on my ass from when I landed on the asphalt during the Rollerblading debacle.

"I'm glad you all were sitting in here enjoying the musical stylings of Ms. Julie Andrews. I just bit it on the hill and almost got hit by a car."

"Are you okay?" my father asked.

"What do you care?" I replied. "My ass hurts." That was the first, but certainly not the last time I uttered those words.

"Well," my father said opening the hallway closet door, "lucky for you, I have this inner tube from when I got my hemorrhoids removed a few months ago. If your ass hurts that much, you can just sit on this."

"Sit on this!" I said as I gave my father the finger after he turned away from me.

"KIDS!" my stepmother yelled from the other room, "it's time to bake a cake for your father."

The last thing I wanted to do was bake my father a cake. I needed about twelve Tylenol and a heating pad for my ass. My stepmother went into the kitchen and gathered all of the materials that we would need to make a cake. Then she left the room.

"Have at it, kids," she said as she exited.

"What?" I asked. "You're seriously leaving an eight- and eleven-year-old in the kitchen to make a cake?"

"Uh-huh," she said. She was trying to kill us. Seconds later, my brother disappeared. I guess it would be up to me to make my father's birthday cake.

I decided I was going to do the other thing that I did best: ruin someone else's birthday. By age eleven, I hated attention being put upon anyone other than me. My father's birthday was the tip of the iceberg. For some reason, I was an attention-seeking little brat who hated celebrating any occasion that did not involve me. Pair that with the fact that my stepmother had just tried to kill me again, and I knew what I had to do. I looked around the kitchen and decided that I was going to make the most disgusting cake anyone had ever tasted. I looked under the sink and found a bottle of Drano. The thought of poisoning everyone quickly popped into my mind. I then realized that I had horrible short-term memory loss and would probably forget that I had poisoned the cake in the first place and indirectly kill myself in the process. Besides, that would have been a waste of a perfectly good cake.

As I considered ways to either kill my family or give them all food poisoning, I glanced into the living room to see my father, stepmother, and brother watching *Mary Poppins*. I love a good Julie Andrews film more than anything in the world and wondered why I was the one who had to make my father's stupid cake. I looked at my stepmother, who glanced back at me with a look that said, "You better make that cake, bitch!"

I put the cake ingredients into a bowl, mixed the contents, and put it into a pan, sans Drano. In lieu of joining my family I decided to eat a whole bag of chips on the kitchen floor and wait for the cake to finish baking. We had decided as a family to make my father a Funfetti cake, my favorite kind. It's just a vanilla cake with sprinkles in it, but I can't get enough of them.

As I waited, I overheard my family singing the wrong lyrics to "A Spoonful of Sugar."

It's "Every task you undertake becomes a piece of cake," you fucking morons! I thought.

Ding! My cake was ready. I put my oven mitts on and took my delicious-looking Funfetti cake out of the oven. In lieu of joining my family, I decided to eat a whole bag of Combos on the kitchen floor and wait for the cake to finish cooling.

After a few minutes of waiting for the cake to cool, it was time to ice it. I mixed regular icing with sprinkles and applied it to the cake. Once I was finished, I delighted in my latest culinary creation. I had come a long way in the cake-making department from a few years ago when I had made my mother a cake using only crayons, glue, thumb tacks, and frosting. I then glanced back into the living room to see my family as they continued watching the movie. They looked so happy. Kind of like a Hallmark card. A Hallmark card from hell, that is. I decided that I was going to stop being such a bratty little kid and join them for the end of the film. "Let's Go Fly a Kite," after all, brings joy into everyone's heart. Suddenly, the spirit of Mary Poppins was inside of me, and I couldn't possibly go through with ruining my father's birthday cake. That wouldn't be fair of me—Mary herself would agree with that. How could I ever watch that glorious film again if I couldn't retain its message of tolerance for others and fabulous tea parties on the ceiling? Even though my father had married Satan's mistress, it was not my place to destroy his dreams of having the perfect birthday cake.

I put all of my baking tools away and glanced at the beautiful cake I had just finished baking. It looked glorious. I would have to wait until after dinner to eat it, which I found ridiculous considering I had just eaten not only a whole bag of chips, but

Combos as well. I turned around to exit the kitchen and must have tripped on my fatness or something, because before I knew it, I was going down. For one reason or another I tried grabbing the table, but grabbed the plate that the cake was sitting on. As I hit the floor, I had taken the cake with me and before I knew it, my father's birthday cake went flying up in the air and landed right on my head.

"What's going on in there?" my father asked as he entered the kitchen.

"I FELL," I yelled, "and your cake landed on my head!"

"GET OFF OF THE FLOOR!" my stepmother yelled.

I was covered in cake.

"AND STOP EATING CAKE OFF THE FLOOR!" my father yelled.

"I'm sorry, Dad," I said as I got up.

"You did this on purpose," my stepmother cried.

"No," I replied, "ruining everyone's life is more your MO than mine."

My stepmother grunted. What a bitch.

I had inadvertently ruined my father's birthday cake. After channeling Mary Poppins and realizing that torching someone else's birthday dreams was not the right thing to do, I had unintentionally done it anyway. Not only did my ongoing feud with my stepmother continue, my father insisted that we go out for Chinese food afterward, thus furthering my association with Chinese food and disastrous family events. What did we learn from that fateful afternoon of culinary calamities? Not one thing—except a killer recipe for Funfetti cake that I still use to this day.

HEAVYWEIGHTS

Our heroine overcame having to Rollerblade, but what followed was more shocking than Kimberly coming back from the dead on *Melrose Place*. Stacey threw another wrench into Mark's game plan. He was at an age when children are supposed to be figuring out who they are going to be as adults (or in his case, how gay they are going to be). What you are about to read is disturbing on many levels. Will our beloved chanteuse survive the horrors of Camp Hell, or will evil prevail?

It was time to put away our boas and capes. Alas, the final day of theater camp was upon us.

"Oh my God, I can't believe it's our last day of camp!" I said to my buddy Jesse as I hugged him. I was wearing my autographed T-shirt from the musical *The Secret Garden*. For the past two summers, I had attended a theater camp in New Rochelle, New York, called Stagedoor. It was the most amazing place in the world. I got to be as gay as I possibly could without anyone from my family seeing me, making fun of me, or punching me in the throat. The summer after sixth grade, I left Stagedoor vowing to return next year and get the lead in the main stage show. Rumors were flying that the camp had gotten the rights to perform *West Side Story* and it had been a twelve-year lifelong dream of mine to play Tony. However, I was grossly overweight, so I promised my camp friends I would come back next summer half the man I used to be. But before I went all Nirvana on everyone's ass, I parted ways with the people who had become my closest friends in only three weeks.

"Bye, Jesse," I said as we hugged. "I'll miss you terribly." Oh, the dramatics of theater camp good-byes. Jesse was my best friend at Stagedoor that summer. We performed in a show together and while backstage one night, he laid one on me. It was my first man-on-man kiss and it was magical. I told Jesse that we would have to keep in touch until we reunited at camp next summer. I was devastated to part ways with my new best friend of three weeks, but knew if we kept in touch, it would only be a mere forty-nine weeks before we met again. We said good-bye and I got on my flight back to D.C., hoping that when I returned everyone would be cooler than when I left. Nope!

"Mark!" my father said as I got off the plane and entered the airport. "We are so glad you are back!"

I hugged my father. I guess I was glad to see him.

"I thought Stacey was going to be with you when you picked me up," I said, questioning where my evil stepmother was. Perhaps they had divorced while I was away and she had crawled back into the hole from whence she came.

"She's in the car, smoking," my father replied. No such luck.

"You look..." my father trailed off. I think he was expecting me to magically lose a million pounds while I was away at camp. I guess he had forgotten that I was away at theater camp, where the most exercise I got was making out with Jesse.

"What?" I asked.

"You look ... healthy," my father said. "What happened to those tennis lessons you had planned on attending?"

"Well, I actually didn't touch a ball all summer." Though I had come close. "I just got caught up with the show, I really didn't have time for tennis. Besides, I was the *only* one who signed up for them and I didn't want the other kids to think I was a total loser."

My father looked defeated. Everything he did to try to get me to lose weight backfired and I just kept eating and kissing boys that he didn't know about, none of which helped in my struggle to shed excess pounds.

"We are going to have to put you on a diet, young man," my father said as he grabbed my bags and we headed toward the car.

"Okay," I said. I always tried to humor him. Little did he know I had a stash of goodies on hand for whenever he planned one of his sneak-attack diets.

We walked out of the airport and joined my stepmother, who had been chain smoking cigarettes at a feverish pace while waiting for us in the car. She was such a bitch. She weighed about ninety pounds (eighty of those pounds were from her big fat head) and always had a beef with me. I don't know if it was because I was fat, or because I rocked pleather better than she could, but we did not get along at all. When I got into the car she acknowledged me with a grunt and I grunted back at her. We clearly weren't making any progress in the communication department during this exchange. I hated her and she hated me—lines had been drawn in the sand long ago and both parties knew better than to cross them. I sat in the car and remembered all of the fun times that I had at camp and simply could not wait until next summer when I could return to the only place in the world where I felt comfortable. Assuming my stepmother did not push me out of a window between now and then, I was good to go.

The next few months passed uneventfully. I kept in contact with Jesse and we wrote each other about four times a week. He wrote me that November and told me that his mother had caught him masturbating in his bathroom and hadn't spoken to him since. My mother found this letter and began asking questions about my relationship with Jesse.

"Who is this Jesse fellow again?" my mother asked.

"A friend from camp," I replied. "We hung out all summer."

"Is he gay?"

"I don't know," I said. What the fuck, I was like twelve. I wasn't really sure if I was gay, let alone this kid. I did know he had an affinity for Diana Ross and the color pink. But so did I, so I wasn't sure what the big deal was. "What's with the questions?"

"Well, when you're away over the summer I get very worried. I just want to make sure that the people that you are hanging out with while you're gone are legit." God love her.

"Everyone is fine. During the three weeks one spends at summer camp, lifelong friends are made and dreams are shattered, Mother. Don't you know these things?" Clearly, my dramatic skills from the summer hadn't waned.

"All right, but if anything ever happens while you are away, you call me!"

"Mom, it's fine. Relax, it's November. I'm not going any-where until next summer anyway."

When December rolled around I got an urgent letter from Jesse telling me that I needed to make a beeline to the nearest multiplex to see what he proclaimed was "the movie of our gen-eration." *"It's called* Clueless. *I have already seen it seven times and I know you are going to just love it!"* he wrote.

I had never heard of it but was always game to see a new movie. Jesse said that he absolutely loved it and since we both loved Diana Ross, why would our tastes in movies be any dif-ferent?

A few days later, I stole away into the night in a pair of sunglasses and a wig from the Burt Reynolds wig collection. I knew I was going to see a movie that most twelve-year-old boys wouldn't be caught dead viewing and had to be incognito. I went to the theater, sat down, and watched one of the most incredible movies ever made. The girls were fabulous and wore fabulous clothes. The guys were cute and dressed really well and there was a full-on makeover scene in the middle of the film that was to die for. I watched intently. I decided I loved any movie with a makeover scene. I took everything in. I memorized the hilarious quotes, especially the ones talking about "the Valley." I had no idea what the Valley was, but it sounded amazing. Two hours later, I was a different man. I was gay. *Clueless* had confirmed it.

I left the theater missing Jesse. *Clueless* made me think of him so much because I knew that he was the only other person in the world who would appreciate such cinematic genius as that.

The holidays were around the corner and when my father asked me what I wanted, I had a full list of demands.

"Well, first off, I absolutely need the soundtrack from *Clueless*," I said.

"What the hell is *Clueless*?" my father asked.

"Only the most amazing movie ever made," I replied as I rolled my eyes. Didn't he know these things? Had he been living under a rock?

"Is that like *Clue*?" he asked. Another incredible film, but not what I was going for at that point.

"As if!" I replied.

"As if what?"

"Jesus! I will find it at the store and you can buy it," I continued. "I also need a bottle of cologne from *Melrose Place*."

"Melrose Place in L.A.?"

"No, the television show, duh!"

"The television show *Melrose Place* has its own cologne line? When did that happen?"

"When do any amazing things happen? They just happen, Dad, it's life."

"I don't know about any of this," my father said. "You've changed."

Considering the previous year he had purchased a signed poster from the Broadway show *Guys and Dolls* for me as a Hanukah present, these gift demands seemed about on par with what my interests had been up to that point.

"Okay, I guess I can get these things for you," he said. "But don't you want a new baseball cap or something?"

"Uh, sounds nice, but that doesn't really go with the motif of my winter/spring ninety-six collection," I replied.

"Motif?" he asked.

"Yes, it's going to be a new and improved me in 1996!"

"Does that new and improved you mean that you are going to change your eating habits?"

"Nope. Everything in that department stays the same. But I need a new look, don't you think?" I had been rocking my older brother's worn-out fraternity T-shirts. Any look besides that was going to be an improvement. Around then my asshole stepmother entered the room. She was probably smoking a cigarette or yelling at someone on the phone or something. I may seem as if I am taking some artistic liberties when describing her, but she is truly an evil and horrible person. But at that juncture in our relationship her depravity was just beginning to blossom.

"I overheard your conversation," she said in my general direction. "Were those boys you were hanging out with at camp gay?"

"Don't talk to me," I replied. I attempted to converse with the woman as little as possible, but my father was probably trying to get some that night so he said, "Answer your stepmother."

"I don't fucking know," I replied.

"LANGUAGE!" my father yelled.

"Listen lady, I am twelve. I think it's a bit early to be making generalizations about my peers' sexuality at such a tender age."

They both just looked at me. I was *such* a smart-ass, neither one of them ever knew what to do with me. My stepmother looked at me and in her eyes I saw the venom of a thousand poisonous snakes. She had her idea of what boys should and shouldn't be doing. I believe that was when she hatched her plan to destroy me once and for all.

The rest of the school year went off effortlessly. The highlight was being cast in the school production of *The Music Man*.

It was an amazing event, which in my mind was to lead up to my monumental return to Stagedoor, a better performer, but still as fat as ever. I could pull off Tony—they had no idea what they were in for. I had taken every dance class and singing lesson I could afford and was going to rock the auditions that summer. In May I went to my father's house to fill out what I thought were forms for the classes I wanted to take at Stagedoor that summer. I was so excited to be returning to the camp where I felt I could be myself. I had mailed Jesse a letter earlier that week telling him how fabulous camp was going to be that summer and that I secretly hoped we would go to second, which wasn't much of a secret if I told him about it. However, he had just bleached his hair, and I wasn't sure how I was going to feel about his new look. When my dad and stepmother put the paperwork in front of me, I noticed the letterhead read Hidden Crest and not Stagedoor.

"What the hell is this?" I asked.

"Your stepmother and I felt that it was time for you try a different camp," my father said.

"Oh really?" I replied. "Wasn't it her idea to send me to Stagedoor in the first place?" It was. However, the only reason that she sent me to camp was because it got my little brother and me out of the house during part of the summer, although Kevin went to an all-boys sports camp in Maine and I sashayed off to Stagedoor. Those were the months the court said we were supposed to be spending with my father. She did not want us around; therefore, she did it to benefit herself.

"Yes it was," the evil whore said. "But now I—I mean we—think it's best for you to move on. The boys at your old camp were a little—"

"Different," my father interrupted. "They were a little different. We think it's time for you to be around other boys your age and . . . well . . . play sports."

"Seriously?" I asked.

"Yes," my father replied. "It will be wonderful. It's a basketball camp. An all-boys basketball camp."

Words such as *basketball* were not in my vocabulary. My father gave a pantomime demo on what the sport involved and I wanted no part of it.

"You did this!" I screamed at my stepmother, "and you will pay!" I said as I ran out of the room. Earlier that year, Blair had pushed Téa out of a window on *One Life to Live*. I hoped that life was about to imitate art in my house. All I needed to do was find a big window and throw that bitch out of it. I'd try to get off on a technicality, like temporary insanity. I was only twelve, but I was willing to risk it, and knew with the right amount of makeup and a good old-fashioned crooked lawyer, I would probably be able to.

"WHAT THE FUCK?" my mother yelled into the phone the next day. "Mark loved that theater camp, and you are sending him to . . . basketball camp? Really?"

My mother, forever my champion, was livid that my father had switched things up behind her back. She realized that I belonged at Stagedoor and that a chimpanzee would have fared better at a basketball camp than me. I sat there and watched my mother go off on my father over the phone. As I listened to their conversation, I began to wonder if there was something really wrong with me. There must have been if my father and evil stepmother would go to such great lengths to literally turn my life upside down. It wasn't until later in life that I realized, I had it right all along.

"Well," my mother said as she hung up the phone, "it looks like you're screwed."

"Why?" I asked.

"Your asshole of a father put down a fifteen-thousand-dollar, nonrefundable deposit on the camp, so you have to go or he is out a ton of money."

"I have to?"

"You should go," she said. "He's an asshole, but that's a lot of money and he wants to help you ... I think." It seemed as though we were both confused as to whom this camp was actually helping.

"Okay, but if he wants to help me and thinks I am gay, why in the world would he send me to an all-boys camp?"

"He's an idiot. Plain and simple."

"I don't know anything about this camp. I don't even know where it is," I said.

"It's outside of Boston. In New Hampshire."

"New Hamp ... shire?" This state was clearly not on my radar.

"Yes, New Hampshire. It's only a month, Mark. Maybe it will be fun."

"Well, Mother," I said, "we all thought that Kimberly blowing up Melrose Place was going to be fun and look at what a mess that turned out to be!"

It turns out, there are places worse than D.C. after all. Hidden Crest, New Hampshire, for example, is one of them. Located near Dartmouth College, Hidden Crest is a quaint and dreary lakeside town where the devil and his children set up shop and called it a summer camp. As my father and stepmother dropped me off in this fresh hell, I finally mustered up the courage to use a word that I had been waiting to drop at just the right occasion.

"CUNT!" I yelled at my stepmother.

"MARK!" my father yelled.

"That's what she is. She is a cunt. And the worst part is, she knows it."

My stepmother just stood there and smiled at me. She was probably thinking about how she was going to poison my father, get away with it, and steal all of his money while I was gone at camp.

"I HATE YOU!" I yelled at my father. "But I hate her more!"

"Why me?" the devil whisperer questioned.

"BECAUSE THIS WAS ALL YOUR IDEA!" I yelled at the top of my lungs. Other parents dropping their children off began to casually eavesdrop on our conversation as they sent their children on their way. I continued at foghorn level: "I'm not even your son; I don't know why you even care. Why can't you just let me do what I want to do? I wasn't hurting anyone."

"Because you are not acting how a boy is supposed to act," she replied.

"Oh, and you know so much about how boys are supposed to act, don't you?" I said. "You don't even know how women your own age are supposed to act. Someone who drinks as much, smokes as much, and takes as many pills as you do should not be telling anyone how to act!" Had I been about ten years older, the two of us would have most likely been the best of friends due to her bad habits. She's pretty much everything I look for in a friend in adulthood, but at twelve, I hated her.

"YOU'RE SUCH A BRAT!" my stepmother yelled.

"Oh yeah?" I said. "I may be a brat, BUT YOU'RE STILL A CUNT!" I was so incredibly loud that everyone around us stopped dead in their tracks. Had this been a cartoon, an elderly woman would have said, "My word," as her monocle dropped into her champagne glass. I wondered where the hell Kimberly was. Couldn't she have blown up my stepmother instead of my beloved Heather Locklear?

"Hello," a man said as he came up behind me.

"HOLY SHIT!" I yelled. He scared me. He came at me like the Flash, but when I turned around a small, sixty-something-year-old man was standing there, wearing a Polo shirt with a monogrammed H on it. I was hoping the H stood for *Hello, Dolly!,* a production that was possibly in the works for later in the summer, but much to my chagrin, it stood for Hidden Crest. I turned around again to see what my father and stepmother were up to, but when I looked behind me all I saw was a cloud of smoke. They had driven away so quickly and without a proper good-bye that I felt abandoned. Kind of like how Dumpster prom babies must feel.

"Welcome to Hidden Crest," the man said. "You must be Mark. I'm Carl. I hear you are not very happy to be here?"

"What tipped you off? The fact that I just called my step-mother a cunt or the fact that I am currently planning an escape route in my head right now?"

"Oh, there is no escaping Hidden Crest, my friend," Carl said eerily. "There isn't a town around here for miles. You'll be walking a mighty long time to find anyone to help you."

"I'll find a way—just you wait." Clearly my smart-ass she-nanigans were not going to fly here. If I was going to escape, I was going to have to befriend everyone, then turn on them.

"Let me show you around," Carl said. The first stop was the cafeteria, a place I hoped to be spending a majority of the summer.

The camp owner showed me around the cafeteria as he chatted about the food.

"It's all very healthy for you. Everything is cooked to order. Lean meats, vegetables, everything a caveman would have eaten. No pastas, no starches, etcetera."

He was omitting the best parts. "Wait...What?" I asked. "What kind of desserts do you serve? Pineapple upside-down cake? Funfetti cake? Cupcakes? Some form of cake, please, God, tell me you have cake!"

"No cakes here. We serve fruit for dessert."

I had officially entered Nazi Germany. Stagedoor always offered cake for dessert. None of the eating-disorders-to-be ever partook in such offerings, but I always ate whatever they didn't want.

"What the hell kind of operation are you running here?"

"It's a healthy camp for boys," Carl said.

"Is it...?" I couldn't bear to say the words myself, "...a..."

"It's not a fat camp," he said.

"FAT CAMP? Oh my God!" I put my hands to my face and began to weep. My all-time favorite movie as a child was *Heavyweights*, a movie about fat kids who were sent to Camp Hope to lose weight. You know that feeling you get the moment you realize something is hilarious until it's actually happening to you? Like when you're watching *Weekend at Bernie's* and you're thinking: *Wow, this movie is hilarious! I wish I was spending every weekend with Bernie.* However, if you had to cart a dead guy around for an entire weekend while pretending he was alive it would be not only not funny but gross, exhausting, and illegal. That was my moment.

The difference between this camp and the camp from *Heavyweights* was that there were very few fat people at this camp. A majority of the campers were returnees who wanted to keep their weight off. The owner of the camp sent me off to my cabin, where I promptly put the *Clueless* soundtrack into my portable CD player and began reading from cover to cover the *Soap Opera Digest* I had bought at the airport. I was about to miss my stories for a full month. I had to make sure there was something, anything, to keep me connected to what was going on.

I slept for about two days until someone had the nerve to wake me up.

"Hello," a kid yelled as he poked me with a stick. "Hello, it's Jeremy. Your bunkmate. It's time to wake up. You've been sleeping for an awfully long time."

"OH SHIT!" I yelled.

"What is it?" Jeremy asked.

"It wasn't a dream. I'm living a nightmare," I said.

"What are you talking about?" Jeremy asked.

"I thought my coming to this awful place was a dream, but it turns out it's not. I am really here," I said.

"I'm supposed to be singing show tunes all summer long, not attempting to lose weight with you, Poindexter."

"You could stand to lose a few," Jeremy said as he gave me the once-over.

"Mind your business," I replied. "It's bad enough that my idiot father told me this was basketball camp. Now I'm being told it's a backward-ass fat camp. I'll tell you what, kid, as this web of lies continues to untangle, it's very reminiscent of when Michael found out that Sydney was a prostitute on *Melrose Place*. That didn't end very well, and I'm pretty sure this won't either."

"Come on," Jeremy said. "I promise you'll have fun."

"As if!"

"As if what?"

"Never mind," I said. I hadn't eaten in about two days and I was starving. "Can we eat?"

"Yes, it's time for breakfast," Jeremy said. "Change your clothes and let's go. If you want to take a shower, you can walk down the path to the showers." I certainly needed something. Mosquitoes had violated my body while I slept, and I was itching everywhere.

"Showers? As in the plural of a shower?"

"Yes," he replied, "everyone showers together."

Gay.

"I don't think I have the strength to shower right now, because I am so incredibly hungry, so let's eat." There was no way I was going to shower with a bunch of guys. What would happen if I got excited? Then all the boys would know I was a homo. However, none of the other boys rolled into camp with a bottle of *Melrose Place* cologne, which would have clearly tipped anyone off, but that was safely put away, with my *Soap Opera Digest* in the bottom of my suitcase. I was going to have to change my ways in order to fit in. I felt like Demi Moore in *G.I. Jane*. She had to change her ways to fit in with the boys in the army. However, shaving my head was out of the question.

Jeremy took me down to the cafeteria and we ate a healthy breakfast of soggy oatmeal and bananas. Day one and I hated it already. But Jeremy was lovely. He was super cute and super fit. He was an "after," meaning he had already lost weight and came back because he actually liked it and wanted to keep the weight off. When he was telling me all of this I felt as if he was speaking Mandarin, because everything he said made absolutely no sense to me whatsoever. But he was a funny kid. He would try to tell jokes and fuck up the ending, so every joke ended with: "Oh, no, what I meant to say was . . . and that's why that joke is supposed to be funny."

"Jeremy, honey," I said, as if I were Joan Collins on *Dynasty,* though I would have been smoking a candy cigarette instead of a real one, "a joke isn't funny if you say 'and that's why the joke is supposed to be funny.' It's just supposed to be funny. And that wasn't." They never were, but Jeremy gave me the lay of the land and showed me where everything was.

That afternoon was water sports afternoon where everyone would team up with a buddy and do an activity on the lake. I had asked if there was a swimming pool to lounge around by and possibly get some sun, but was informed there was no pool, just a crib, a roped-off section, in a dirty lake to swim in. In my usual fashion of being a lazy fat-ass, I had already befriended the nurse, who was the only woman on the campus, and told her my story. Her name was Leslie and we bonded over a mutual love of *One Life to Live.* She had a TV in her nurse's office, so I figured I would be seeing a lot of her that summer. Having read *Soap Opera Digest* earlier in the week, I knew Carlo Hesser was strolling back into Llanview that Friday, so I had to plan some sort of ailment to take place around two in the afternoon, one central time, later that week. But that day, with storm clouds looming, I thought about faking an illness to get out of doing any sort of physical activity. It was past three in the afternoon, enough time to catch the tail end of *General Hospital* if I left then, but I figured it may be best to stick this one out and save the dramatics of faking an ailment for a more important time, such as having to run track or something ridiculous like that. Jeremy suggested that we get into a canoe and row around the lake. I had never been in a canoe before, but he assured me he would spearhead the operation.

We both got into the canoe but the water was looking a bit choppy. We swayed back and forth as we entered and sat on the wooden slabs inside. God love Jeremy for knowing what the hell was going on, because immediately I almost tipped us over. I wasn't the best of swimmers because when I was in the water I looked more like a piece of muffin floating in a cup of coffee. I would just float around and embrace my fatness. This canoe was a foreign object to me and the two of us did not get along. How had I come to this? All I wanted to do that summer was grow bangs and lovingly sing "Something's Coming" to a white girl pretending to be Puerto Rican. What the hell happened?

As we began canoeing around the lake, a man in a speedboat approached us. He had a few kids in his boat with him and at first I thought he might be taking everyone to the MTV beach house.

"HEY, JEREMY!" the man yelled.

"GLENN!" Jeremy yelled back at the camp counselor.

"Who the hell is that?" I asked. Glenn looked like a douche bag. He was wearing sunglasses, when he clearly needed nothing to block his eyes from the absent sun. He was shirtless, had a beard that was reminiscent of something a rapist would sport, and was just all around gross looking. He really looked like one of those guys who just randomly showed up at girls' high-school basketball games for no apparent reason.

"CIRCLE AROUND US AND MAKE OUR CANOE ROCK!" Jeremy yelled.

"Ummm . . . how about not?" I asked.

"Come on, Mark, it'll be fun. Like we're in a whirlpool."

"I am fine just gliding around the lake, thank you very much."

But Jeremy didn't listen and Glenn began circling around our canoe with the intent to kill. Some people should never be allowed in the same room as a child, let alone counsel them at a summer camp. Glenn was one of those people. He continued to circle our canoe and we began swaying back and forth.

"Seriously, he needs to stop," I told Jeremy.

"We'll be fine," Jeremy said as our canoe tipped over.

This was the second time in two years that my life flashed before my eyes. Two near-death experiences in less than twenty-four months at the hands of my diabolical nemesis: Stacey. I started blaming her for everything, even when she wasn't there. Underwater, I quickly began to contemplate whether or not to fight. Could I possibly go through another month of agonizing torture or should I just call it a day and die now? Nothing fun was going to happen this summer and I had had a pretty good run, so why not just throw in the towel? I had managed to see every episode of *Melrose Place*, so why fight it?

"MARK!" I heard Jeremy yell from above.

How was he already back in the canoe? I wondered.

I floated to the top and began bobbing up and down in the water.

"Wasn't that fun?" Jeremy asked.

"NO!" I yelled. "Eating all day and watching reruns of *Knots Landing* is fun. This is torture."

"CLIMB BACK INTO THE CANOE," Jeremy yelled.

Glenn, who was sitting in the speedboat next to us, decided to chime in: "Use your upper-body strength to hoist yourself back into the canoe."

"Upper-body strength? What upper-body strength?"

I put both of my hands onto the ledge of the canoe and

tried to hoist myself up and back into it. Unfortunately, the only workout my arms had gotten in my twelve years on earth was from putting chip to mouth, and that doesn't really build one's biceps.

"Come on, Mark, you can do it," Glenn said.

"Shut the fuck up," I said under my breath.

I pulled up with my arms and could not manage to maneuver myself back into the canoe. After about ten tries, it took Glenn and three of the kids on the speedboat to get me back into the canoe. I didn't know if these kids were actually going to the MTV beach house, but thank God they were there and well-toned or I would have been a goner.

Jeremy and I rowed back to shore and I immediately made a beeline to my only ally for miles.

"LESLIE!" I yelled as I flung open the doors to the nurse's office.

"Mark, what's the matter?" she said as I ran to her.

"My canoe tipped over. That asshole Glenn did it. I think I have a concussion and will most certainly need to go home."

"Let me take a look at you," Leslie said as she inspected my head. I glanced over at the TV to possibly catch the last ten minutes of *General Hospital,* but much to my displeasure, *Oprah* had already started. "You look okay to me."

"DAMN IT!" I yelled. "I hate this fucking place! Why am I here and not at home baking cupcakes and watching old movies? This summer is going to blow."

"Maybe you need to change your attitude a little bit," Leslie said.

"Change my attitude? Maybe these people need to go fuck themselves. And that Carl is the worst of them all."

"You're telling me," Leslie said. I wondered what beef she had with the camp owner, whom everyone else seemed to love.

"Whatever do you mean?" I innocently asked Leslie.

"Well, he just will not seem to ever leave that skanky wife of his."

"Why would you want him to do that?" Could I possibly add extortion to my list of crimes? If Leslie spilled some serious dirt about Carl, I could blackmail his ass into letting me leave camp early. Erica Kane would have been so proud. This is why I watched soap operas in lieu of cartoons as a child—life lessons learned.

"Well," Leslie said, as if she were letting me in on some deep dark secret, "do you remember on *One Life to Live* when Viki decided that she didn't want to be with Clint anymore, so she could begin seeing Sloane?"

"Listen, lady, I have been around the block a time or two myself," I told her. "You're having an affair with Carl, aren't you?"

"Yes," she replied, "but please keep it between the two of us."

"Of course," I said with a grin as big as a Cheshire cat's. "One question."

"Yes."

"You are so much cuter than he is, so why do you even care?"

"Because, Mark," she replied. I began wondering why anyone over the age of eighteen even bothered telling me anything. I was such a troublemaker. She continued, "When you meet the one, you just know."

"What about his wife?" I asked.

"That whore," she laughed. "No competition for me whatsoever." I believed her. She was pretty smoking and about thirty years younger than what I imagined Carl's wife to be.

"Good luck with that," I said as I walked out of the nurse's office stealing a few Band-Aids on my way out.

As I walked back to my cabin, I decided to concoct a diabolic plan to escape from camp by ruining several lives, while I came out of the entire situation relatively unscathed. I would be here for another two or three days, tops, and then off I would go, back to D.C. However, when I returned to my cabin, things went from bad to worse. I flung the screen door open and noticed that there were a few new guests at the camp. I figured that Jeremy and I were not going to be alone in our spacious cabin all summer, but did not think that we would be rooming with the Model UN.

"¡Hola!" kid number one said.

"Uh, hey," I said.

"Mark, come meet our new roommates," Jeremy said as he gestured the four new recruits to Camp Hell toward me. "This is Anthony," he said as I shook Anthony's hand. "And this is Anthony," Jeremy said as he gestured toward the other Italian-looking kid.

"So wait, you're both named Anthony?" I asked.

"Fuck you," Anthony 1 said.

"Fuck you," Anthony 2 said.

They both looked at me like I had just sharted in front of them.

"They don't speak English. They're Italian, and only seem to know English curse words for some reason," Jeremy explained.

"VA FANGOOL!" I yelled. The Italians looked at me as if I had just killed their parents. "Well, seems as though you can dish it out, but you can't take it."

Jeremy gestured to two more foreign kids.

"This is Giovanni," Jeremy said as I shook Giovanni's hand. "And this is Juan," he said as I shook Juan's hand.

"Do any of them speak any English?" I asked.

"I don't think so," Jeremy replied.

"What the hell are they doing here?" Anthony squared and Giovanni seemed to be from Italy, but I wasn't really sure where Juan was from. Somewhere in Poor, I imagined.

"Apparently, it's cheaper for them to go to camp in America or something. I think it's nice. Maybe we can learn about another culture while we are here."

"Are you like a real person, Jeremy?" I asked. "You are way too happy. You must be hiding some sort of deep dark secret or something. I have never met anyone as happy as you are."

"I don't know. I just like people I guess," he replied.

"Well, that makes one of us," I said. Suddenly things went from worst to agonizingly torturous when Glenn waltzed into our bunk.

"HEY CAMPERS," Glenn yelled.

"GLENN!" all of the foreigners yelled. They couldn't say hello in English, but they apparently knew exactly who Glenn was. Curious. "So listen, guys, Jack was supposed to be the counselor for this bunk, but he was arrested for sleeping with underage girls or something, so looks like you're stuck with me."

"JESUS CHRIST!" I yelled. Everyone looked at me.

"Something the matter, little man?" Glenn asked.

"I have to see Carl," I said as I breezed out the door. I made a beeline for the head cottage to take down Carl, ruin his marriage, and get the hell out of Dodge as quickly as possible.

I sashayed across camp as fast as my cookie-loving ass

could go. I hustled through the woods, and on the other end I saw a light that guided me toward Carl's cottage. I could tell that he was home and walked up the stairs to his cottage and knocked on the door.

"Oh, hello, young man," Carl said as he opened the door.

"I'm coming in," I said. I barged in and took a seat on one of the big sofas he had. Compared to the shit shacks the rest of us were staying in, Carl's cottage looked like the Taj Mahal.

"Can I help you with something?" Carl asked.

"Shut the door," I said. If there was one thing I had learned from Erica Kane, it was to make sure that no one else was around while you were hatching an extortion plot. If someone happens to overhear, then they can blackmail you and the cycle continues.

"Is something wrong?" Carl asked as he shut the door and came to sit on the sofa adjacent to me.

"I was just speaking to Leslie," I said as cool as a cucumber, "and found out something relatively shocking." I glanced at the picture of his wife and children on the table by his sofa. What a loving family they had. Certainly he would not want to give that up for a summer fling with the camp nurse.

"Oh, and what was that?" he questioned.

"She told me that you two had a little something going on."

"ARE YOU SERIOUS, YOUNG MAN?" he yelled.

"Yes."

"GET OUT!" he screamed.

"Why? I am here to make a little bargain with you." My first-ever extortion plot was going off better than I could ever have hoped. I had him right where I wanted him.

"I am not making any sort of deal with a twelve-year-old," he said.

"I think you will want to, once you know what my offer is,"
I replied.

"Offer? WHAT ARE YOU TALKING ABOUT?" Carl
yelled. "Were you raised by wolves?"

"No, I was raised by Susan Lucci and Heather Locklear. If
you have a problem with that, you can take it up with them!"

"What do you want?" he asked.

"Okay. I promise not to tell your wife about your tryst with
the nurse if you let me go home."

"No deal."

"What? You didn't even think about it."

"I did. But, what you didn't think about was how you were
going to get in touch with my wife. She runs the girls camp,
across the lake in Vermont. The only way to get there is by boat,
and judging from your little nautical adventure earlier today, I
don't think you will be up for making that trip."

Son of a bitch.

"I can write her."

"You don't know the address."

"I will find it."

"Listen, you little asshole," he said as he grabbed me by the
collar, "you will tell no one about this. Do you hear me?"

"Excuse me," I said as I backed away from him. "Are you
manhandling me right now?"

"OF COURSE I AM!" he yelled. "You're trying to blackmail me!"

"I want out, Carl. And I want out now," I said.

"Well, sorry buddy boy. I am going to do everything in my
power to make sure that you stay here for the duration of the
summer and I will make your life a living hell."

"Are you threatening me?" I asked.

"No, that's a promise."

"Fine. I will write my mother and tell her what's going on. She'll come and get me."

"Assuming she gets your letters."

"Tampering with other people's mail is a federal offense," I replied. It is. I saw Erica try to steal Brooke's mail earlier that year on *All My Children,* so it must have been true.

"GET OUT!" he yelled. "I don't want to see you for the rest of the summer!"

I stormed out of the cottage and it began to rain. Instead of getting out of camp, I had unleashed a hell that was going to terrorize me for the rest of the summer. My only ally, Leslie, was sure to never speak to me again, as I had outed her secret. To top it all off, I was rooming with four of the five original members of Menudo. I ran back to my bunk, picked up my pen and Winnie-the-Pooh stationery, and began writing my epitaph. Earlier that day I'd realized that my idiotic father and stepmother had given me the wrong address for people to send me mail. First they sent me to this awful place, and now they apparently did not want me to have any contact with the outside world. The following is a real letter that I wrote to my mother. Nothing has been altered from its original format; this is really how crazy (and kind of racist) I was at the age of twelve.

"HELP!" I wrote in big bubble letters on the first page of the letter.

"Mommy—look at this face." I then drew a sad face with a really bad haircut and an arrow pointing to my hair. "My stupid bushy hair which the dumb Hair Cuttery woman gave me."

Not only do I hate camp, I have like 3 or 4 Eye-talians sleeping in my bunk and they curse each other all the time. And besides that, they smell [I wrote the word *smell* with stink lines coming out of it. I was so creative.] They don't have a pool, they have a crib. It's a closed-out part of the lake, which you have to swim in. And as if that's not enough, stupid Dad gave me the wrong address so I'll never get mail. Help! Please! Call me at camp. I want to hear from you. I have 6,000 mosquito bites and I have only been here for three days and I have like 7,000 mosquito bites [apparently the number went up as I was writing the letter]. We don't have a bathroom in our bunk. We have to walk to the bathroom. Last night when I had to piss, I tripped over a branch on my way to the bathroom and felt like an old man. I should have screamed, "Help. I have fallen and I can't get up." There aren't any personal showers so we have to take showers together. (If I come back home smelling bad, you'll know why.) Going to meals is hell too. Dad stayed here for twenty minutes then left—and expected me to hug him. So did Stacey. I hope they both ROT IN HELL. Oh well, but get me out of here. Today the nurse was helping me plot my escape, but now I don't think it's going to work [I couldn't possibly tell my mother that I had tried in vain to blackmail the camp owner]. It would have never worked anyway. Oh well. I love you. Write back. Come and Get Me. Call. Either one—you choose. I love you, Mark.

I was such a scamp. I waited for a night messenger from the U.S. Postal Service to arrive on horseback to take my mail, but when he didn't show, I dropped the letter into the mailbox, in hopes no one would steal it. I went to bed that night and had the most amazing dream that Lorenzo Lamas had spirited me out of camp and back home. When I woke up the next morning to Jeremy's face smiling and telling me to wake up, I knew it couldn't have been true.

"Wake up!" Jeremy said.

"No! Go to hell," I said.

"That's no way to talk to your best camp buddy. Come on, let's shower."

"No. I am not showering with you."

"You'll start to stink," Jeremy said.

"Well, the Italians don't seem to mind, so what do I care? They really aren't frequenting the showers from what I gather either."

"Come on, Mark, you need to take a shower," Jeremy said.

"Like hell I do," I said as I got up, put on my shoes, and walked out the door. As I was walking down to the cafeteria, I glanced by the nurse's office and saw Leslie, who was probably watching *The Price Is Right*, looking extremely melancholy. I hoped that I hadn't gotten her in trouble with that asshole Carl, but then realized she would probably be better off without him. If need be, I would make it a point to pop by later in the day and tell her that she could do better than him and offer a shoulder for her to cry on. For the time being, I needed to get my ass down to the cafeteria and eat something. I was so hungry. Three days of healthy food was taking its toll on me and I was beginning to become weak and possibly anemic. Perhaps it had something to do with the lack of preservatives in my diet or the fact that the cookie food group was now completely lacking from my routine. Either way, I was starving and needed something to eat, and quick.

As I was hiking down the hill, my least favorite person at camp stopped me: Glenn. I am not exactly sure why I hated him as much as I did, but the sight of him made me nauseous. Perhaps it had something to do with the fact that he looked like a straight-up rapist. We were, however, stuck together for the duration of the summer and I was going to have to put up with his nonsense for the rest of the month.

"Where ya going, buddy?" Glenn said as he stopped me.

"I NEED TO EAT. NOW!" I yelled.

"No time for that," Glenn said as he put his hands on my shoulders and physically turned me around and began pushing me back up the hill.

"Are you seriously touching me right now? God only knows where those hands have been," I said. "Where are you taking me? I need to eat something. NOW!"

"Back up the hill," Glenn said. "I got word from Carl this morning—you need to be with the other set of kids at camp."

Oh, shit, they are sending me to be with the fatties, I thought.

"Other kids?" I asked, as Glenn continued to push me back up the hill. "Stop touching me, I can walk up a hill on my own," I added. I was, however, almost completely out of breath and had only walked about ten steps.

"Yes," Glenn said. "Carl thinks it's time for you to be with some of the more proportionally challenged kids at camp."

"The fat kids?" I asked.

"Ummm . . . kind of, yeah."

"DAMN HIM!" I yelled.

I knew it was too good to be true. Granted, I had only been at camp for a few days, and I knew it was only a matter of time before I would be carted away to spend time with the fatter kids at camp. I was, after all, there to lose weight, and until then the only physical exercise I had gotten was being lifted from the cold lake back into a canoe.

"What's your problem with Carl?" Glenn asked as we walked up the hill.

"I hate him. I hate you. And I hate this camp," I replied.

"Okay, understandable," Glenn said.

"What? Aren't you going to tell me that I need to buck up and be a part of the team?"

"No," Glenn replied. "If you don't like it, you don't like it. But remember, it's not forever, and maybe you can learn something here."

"Ummm . . . okay," I replied. That was the first decent thing that had come out of Glenn's mouth in the short time I had known him. We walked up the hill and followed a path that led us behind the community showers (four days in and I still had no idea where they were), through a mess of trees and onto a large playing field. When we approached, all I saw was a bunch of fat-asses. Each was bigger than the next. I was not nearly as fat as these kids were. Was I?

"Okay, Mark," Glenn said, "I have to go back down the hill. I am going to motorboat over to the girls' camp and hopefully motorboat one of the counselors, ha-ha-ha."

What an idiot. Glenn left me, and a waiflike man with glasses and a huge orange Jew-fro approached. At least one of my people was within view.

"I'm Kurt," the redheaded Jew said.

"Mark," I replied.

"I've heard a lot about you from Carl," he said.

Apparently my extortion plot gone wrong was all over the front pages of the *Hidden Crest Tribune* that morning. I was wondering where my copy was and why I had not been interviewed for my side of the story.

"I'm sure," I replied.

"Okay, Mark, we are doing some simple exercises so I can determine what work needs to be done and on whom. This will be quite grueling, but the results will be amazing and maybe you will begin to like yourself again."

"I am pretty amazing just the way I am. Don't you think?" I asked.

He sniffed around me, obviously wondering what intoxicating scent surrounded my body.

"It's cologne. From *Melrose Place*," I said. He looked confused, so I continued. "You know, the TV show." He looked dumbfounded. "But you can buy it at CVS, I think. It's not like from Melrose Place in L.A."

"No cologne. It attracts bugs."

"You're telling me, I have like ten thousand mosquito bites." Apparently I had acquired about three thousand more mosquito bites from when I wrote my mother the night before.

"So don't wear it and you'll be fine," Kurt replied.

"I am trying this new thing," I said.

"Oh, and what's that?"

"I think the French do it."

"What? Not shower and bathe in cologne?"

"Exactly," I replied.

"Well, no more of that. When you are done here, you are going to be dying for a shower."

Doubtful.

Kurt gestured me toward the other fat-asses who were bouncing up and down attempting to do jumping jacks. All I could think about was food. I was so fucking hungry. And thirsty. I would have loved a Coke and was wondering if there was a waitress anywhere nearby. I was also hoping there was one fierce fat girl around who I could talk shit with, but there wasn't one for miles. I watched all of the fatties jump up and down and suddenly realized that the second I joined them, I would be one of them. Perhaps it was time for me to start thinking about my health. I was fat, but was I as fat as the rest of them? As I began weighing in on the rest of the troupe in my head, Kurt began explaining what exactly was going on.

"So what we have here is a test of endurance," Kurt said. I was watching and waiting for the fatties to drop like flies. "We are going to be testing your strength and we are also going to be testing how well you fare during a series of tests."

"Can I please eat something first?" I asked.

"No."

"But I am so hungry."

"They're all hungry too, but they aren't complaining about it."

I looked at the fat boys and all I could see was a look of sheer famishment. They were hungry too. They were just pussies and wouldn't ask for food. But I would start a fat boys' revolution and feed all of us. If Joan of Arc could do it, I certainly could find some hot dogs for these kids.

"Not so much hungry as starving."

"All right, we'll start jumping jacks and we will discuss food later."

"I hate my life," I said as I began jumping jacks with the rest of the fat kids. I did about four and suddenly a bead of sweat rolled down my face. It was something I had never experienced before. The only time I had sweat was while standing in front of an oven, and now here I was doing jumping jacks with twenty fat kids. Seeing the determination in the rest of kids made me think that I could do this after all. If I couldn't beat them, I figured I might as well join them. My constant bitching was clearly not going to get me out of actually working out. As I continued jumping jacks, I noticed that the ground was very soiled. The mud was sticking to my shoe and with each jack I jumped, the muddier my shoe became. I also couldn't help but notice it smelled like my bathroom the day after I realized I had irritable bowel syndrome.

"Excuse me," I said as I stopped jumping. "Uh, Kurt."

"Yes," he said.

"There is some serious mud going on up in here. What's the deal?"

"Oh, that," Kurt replied. "Well, we have been having some plumbing problems at the camp lately and the pipes have backed up onto this field. Not to worry though. Now get back to it."

"So, wait a minute," I said. "This field is filled with crap?"

Kurt said nothing but gave me a look that said, "It's our little secret."

My smart-ass anecdotes were getting me nowhere fast so I simply resumed jumping jacks. I thought about what Jesse and the rest of the kids at Stagedoor were doing. I was pretty certain that they were not playing in their own feces. Instead they were probably listening to Bernadette Peters's new album and wishing I were there with them. I wished I were there. At that point, I wished I were anywhere other than where I was. A hooker hell in Tierra del Fuego sounded like Disney World compared to this place.

Shortly after I finished jumping jacks in my own shit I was told I now needed to do push-ups in my own shit. I looked around and saw that none of the other kids were putting up a fight. Did these kids really want to lose weight? Was I the only one fighting it? My father and stepmother had pounded into my head that I needed to lose weight, so in the spirit of being a badass kid, I naturally did the opposite of what would make them happy. I also wondered if I was the only one who realized that we were playing in our own crap. The boys to my left and right were determined to do as many push-ups as possible and I saw that determination in their eyes. *Good for them,* I thought. All of these thoughts ran through my head as, after a good two minutes went by, I finally had finished doing a push-up. My face almost wound up in shit, but I managed to hoist myself up and back down in less than two minutes. Sweat was dripping from every inch of my body, but it was record time! It took everything I had in me, but I finished it. One whole push-up.

Kurt could see the excruciating pain that we were all in and decided that we had reached our quota for the day.

"Hit the showers, kids," he told us.

I ran as fast as I could back to the nurse's office. I smelled like shit—literally. I opened the door to the nurse's office and noticed that Leslie was nowhere to be found. I turned on her TV in hopes that one of my soap operas would be on, but there was Oprah again, in all of her fat glory.

"DAMN YOU, OPRAH!" I yelled. "You're as fat as a house and everyone listens to what you say. Why does no one listen to me?"

Enraged, I turned the television off and turned around to exit. On my way out, I noticed something I had not seen on my previous trip to the nurse—a telephone. I quickly looked around to see if anyone was around, picked up the phone, and dialed my mother's number.

"DAMN IT!" I yelled when she didn't pick up. It was four o'clock, so I figured she was probably at happy hour with the girls. I then dialed my father's number hoping that someone, anyone, would pick up.

"Hello," the voice on the other end of the phone said.

"Hello. Who is this?" I asked.

"It's Stacey. Who is this?"

"Goddamn it, woman, where is my father?"

"Mark?" she asked. "How are you making a phone call right now? Aren't you at camp?"

"Well, if you must know, you nosy bitch, I broke into the nurse's office and made a long-distance call without anyone knowing. Where's Dad?"

"He's out," she replied. "Having fun yet?" I could just imagine her smirking on the other end.

"I'M IN HELL AND IT'S ALL YOUR FAULT!" I yelled.

She laughed: "I don't know what you mean, my dear."

"Oh, don't pull that shit with me, lady. I've got your number. I will destroy you the second I return from camp. Just you wait."

"I'm sure you will," she replied. "What are you going to do? Quiz me to death with soap opera trivia? Ha-ha-ha."

"I hate you. I hope you die before I get back from camp," I said, not realizing that evil never dies.

"That's not very nice. What would your father say if he heard you talking to me like that?" she asked.

"I hope he dies too. I hope you both die. That's what both of you assholes should get for sending me to this horrible place. Now please tell him I love him and to call me at once!" I slammed the phone down and turned around. A figure stood in the door.

"CARL DUMPED ME!" Leslie yelled.

Goddamn it. I did not have time for this right now.

Leslie was a hysterical mess. She entered her office and sat down in her chair. Suddenly, she stopped crying and began sniffing around.

"What's that smell?" she asked.

"Oh," I replied. "That's me. I smell like shit, I know."

"Take a shower," she replied.

"Uh, I would, but I think you need me right now," I replied, trying to dodge yet another bullet.

"Carl dumped me and now I am all alone," Leslie said.

"You have me," I replied with a smile.

"Thanks Mark, but you're twelve."

"We can still be friends though. I will console you through your hard time."

"You're sweet. But I really cannot talk to you when you smell that way. Please, for the love of God, take a shower."

"Uh, okay," I replied.

"Like, now would be good."

"Okay. I hope you feel better. Find me if you need me," I said as I left her office. Carl was such an asshole, treating my beloved Leslie like that. I wanted to make him pay even more now. I walked back to my bunk, bypassing the shower altogether, and entered. I saw that Anthony 2 was in his bed listening to his headphones. I shot a dirty look at him and lay on my bed. I put the soundtrack from *Clueless* in my portable CD player and began listening. Suddenly, Anthony 2 was standing over me with a CD of his own.

"Janet," Anthony 2 said as he handed me *Design of a Decade: Janet Jackson's Greatest Hits*.

"You?"

"Clueless," I replied. I took my CD out of my CD player and we exchanged discs. God bless the Italians for having good taste in music. I put the disc in and began listening. I skipped to a personal favorite, "Escape," and suddenly was taken away by the music. Before I knew it, I was fast asleep.

"Mark?" a voice said to me.

"Hello? Who's there?" I asked. A portly figure appeared in the doorway. As the figure came closer, I was delighted at who had come to visit me at camp.

"Janet Jackson! Thank God you've come to get me."

"I'm not here to take you away on an escape, Mark. Musically yes, but literally, no." Janet said with her signature half smile, "I'm here to teach you a lesson."

"DAMN IT, JANET!" I yelled. "I am so sick of learning lessons."

"You know, Mark, I have always had trouble with my weight. People in the media have always made backhanded comments about it, but I never let it get me down." She paused. "What's that smell?"

"Oh, it's me. I know, I know, I smell like shit. I was playing in it all day."

"Maybe you should shower," Janet said.

"Maybe you should put out a new record already!" I retorted.

"Listen, Mark, you have a problem with your weight, and I think I can help."

"I know, I'm fat and I don't want to do anything about it. My asshole stepmother is always telling me how fat she thinks I am."

"I've been watching you, Mark," Janet Jackson said. "I like your style. But you do need to lose weight."

"You think?" I said as I looked down at my waistline creating a rippling double-chin effect.

"Yes. It's not healthy to be as heavy as you are at such a young age. When I was on *Good Times*, Florida Evans and I used to have this talk daily. She would always tell me: 'Janet, watch your weight while you're a girl or you'll end up heavy like me.'"

"You know that show really went downhill after they killed John Amos off," I replied.

"Not the point," Janet said. "Wait a second, I didn't come on the show until after John Amos left."

"Whatever," I said. I had no intention of offending Janet Jackson to her face more than once, but James Evans was the glue that held the Evans family together and there was no denying that.

"Anyway, you don't want to get old and have to worry about your weight. There are so many health concerns that come along with it."

"Maybe you're right, Janet," I said, "but my stepmother is such a whore. I kind of want to stay fat just so that bitch doesn't get what she wants."

"Yes, your stepmother is a complete bitch, there is no doubt about that," Janet said, "but, maybe if you lose weight you'll shut her up for good."

"I never thought about it like that, Janet Jackson," I said. I had never thought that the only reason I ever once thought about my weight was because my father and stepmother were constantly bringing it up. I wasn't ready to lose weight because I was being told I needed to, and whenever you're forced into doing something, the results are never what either party intend for them to be. Like how date-rape drugging your girlfriend never works out in anyone's favor so you should just wait until she's ready to put out.

"Just trust me," she said.

"I will, Janet. You and your brother have entertained me

for years. I listen to everything either one of you says. But why didn't you write me back when I asked for a lock of your hair a few years back?"

"Oh that," Janet said. "Well, I was on the Rhythm Nation tour. I was super busy. Here," she said as she yanked a lock of her weave out of her head and handed it to me. "Take this. Lose the weight and prove to that bitch you can do it. And remember, Mark, growing old means giving up everything that gives you any pleasure whatsoever, so cool it with the cookies."

Janet disappeared. In a matter of seconds, Jeremy appeared.

"Janet? Is it you?" I said.

"Janet? Who's Janet?"

"You know, Miss Jackson, if you're nasty."

"What?" Jeremy said.

"Never mind."

It was all a dream.

"It's time for dinner," Jeremy said, sniffing around. "Have you showered? Like, at all since you've been here?"

"I plead the fifth on that one."

"You smell like shit!"

"Yes, yes, yes, I know. I smell like shit. You and everyone else I have encountered today have told me that. I'll shower after dinner."

"I'm sorry, Mark," Jeremy said to me, "but I cannot sit next to you at dinner if you smell like that. You're going to have to sit with the Italians."

It had taken a divine intervention from Janet Jackson, but I finally decided to bite the bullet and get my shit together. I had exactly three weeks left at camp before I got to go home, so I figured I would make the most of it. Besides, exercising wasn't that bad. For the rest of the month of August, I ran, swam, played capture the flag, and even learned how to play basketball. As the summer came to a close, I had never been more excited to get out of a place more and was very happy to not have to be in New Hampshire anymore.

"Bye, Mark," Jeremy said. "I'm really going to miss you. Will you keep in touch?"

"Probably not," I said.

"Well, that's okay," Jeremy replied. "We'll see each other next summer."

"Probably not," I said.

I gathered my things and checked my bags one last time to make sure I had everything, but noticed several important items that I had brought to camp with me were missing.

"WHERE ARE THOSE FUCKING ITALIANS?" I yelled.

"They left already," Jeremy responded.

"They stole my *Clueless* CD and my *Melrose Place* cologne!"

"I'm sure they didn't mean to."

"Jeremy, you need to get a clue. Those Italians have sticky fingers."

I was about to throw something in a fit of rage when Glenn walked in.

"GLENN!" Jeremy yelled. My confusion about everyone's enthusiasm over Glenn continued. I still didn't understand why everyone liked him so much.

"Time to go, kids," Glenn said.

"I'm going to miss you so much," Jeremy said as he hugged Glenn.

"Me too, kiddo," Glenn said. "Ready to go?"

"I've never been more ready for anything in my life," I replied, "and I really hope that I don't see you on a *Dateline* special anytime soon."

Glenn looked dumbfounded. It was a look he had perfected that summer.

I felt like Mary Tyler Moore when she decided to take a job at WJM-TV. I had made it after all. I was ready to go home and got on a flight headed back to Washington, D.C.

"Mark!" my father said as I got off the plane and entered the boarding area.

I hugged my father. I guess I was glad to see him.

"I thought Stacey was going to be with you when you picked me up," I said, questioning where my evil stepmother was. Perhaps they had divorced while I was away and she had crawled back into the hole from whence she came.

"She's in the car, smoking," my father replied. I briefly wondered how long it would be before lung cancer took Stacey from us and started timelining that shit in my head.

"You look amazing," my father said. "It looks like that camp really paid for itself, huh?"

"I guess so," I replied. My father grabbed my bags and we approached the car where my stepmother was waiting for us, chain-smoking. With each step that we took closer to the car, the more my stepmother's eyes lit up. I know that I had convinced myself that I was losing weight to make myself a better person, but the fact that it gave my stepmother pleasure made me irate.

"Mark, you look amazing," she said as I got into the car.

"Thanks, Stacey," I replied. "You're looking a little pasty yourself. Haven't gotten out in the sun much this summer, have we?"

She turned around and exhaled her cigarette smoke in my face. I savored it.

"How much weight have you lost?" Stacey asked.

"About fifteen pounds," I replied.

"Did you make any friends at camp?" my father asked.

"Not a one. I was stuck with this little white kid named Jeremy and three to four Italians. We had nothing in common."

My stepmother finished smoking her cigarette and rolled the windows up. Suddenly, the two of them began sniffing around.

"I haven't showered in a month," I said, as if this was something to be proud of.

"Why not?" my father questioned.

"I don't do communal showers," I responded.

"I can't believe it, Mark," my stepmother chimed in. "You look like a real boy."

"What did I look like before?" I questioned.

"Fat," she said.

"What is wrong with that?"

"Haven't we been over this?" Stacey said. "Boys your age are not supposed to be heavy like that. Or, for that matter, hanging out in the Catskill Mountains singing show tunes."

"There is nothing wrong with singing show tunes," I said.

"Quite frankly, Mark, I think this new and improved you is going to bring this family closer," Stacey said. "I know I like you a lot more." How did my weight determine the closeness of our family?

"Perhaps keeping your hands to yourself would definitely bring this family closer. Your biweekly death threats to my father aren't necessarily Hallmark moments, if you know what I mean," I said.

A wave of anger came over me. In losing fifteen pounds, I

had pleased my stepmother, something I never wanted to do. If my being skinny was going to make her happy, I knew exactly what I needed to do.

Shortly after returning to my mother's house, I made a vow to eat everything in sight for the next two weeks straight. My heart-to-heart with Janet Jackson was all but forgotten, because I planned to gain all of the weight that I had lost before seeing either my father or my stepmother again. Seeing her pleased with me just because I had done what she wanted me to made me want to pull my hair out. There was no way I was going to let that bitch win this round. I even went as far as eating McDonald's, Roy Rogers, and Burger King all in one day. At the end of the two weeks, I had not only gained the fifteen pounds back but had added an extra five.

When I went back to visit my father that weekend, the look on his face was priceless. Stacey was livid, and when asked what had happened to my weight loss, I responded: "Growth spurt. I had a horizontal growth spurt."

My stepmother was furious and our war continued. I think that may have been the night that she tried to stab my father in his sleep, but I cannot recall exactly.

THE FIFTY-DOLLAR DIET

With their fat-camp efforts thwarted, Mark's father
and stepmother were not done with their plot to make
their fat son the perfect boy. Had he not started watching daytime television at such a young age, they may
have gotten their wish, but what happened next was
wrong on so many levels. No one is winning parent of
the year for this next debacle in weight loss.

Your stepmother and I think you are getting a little . . . wide,"
my father said. Since his plan to get me skinny at fat camp
had been thwarted, my father was becoming increasingly dis-
tressed about my weight.

"Wide?" I asked.

"You know . . ." My father drifted off. "Uh, hefty."

My father was obviously disillusioned. Having lived with
my bobble-headed stick figure of a stepmother for several years,
anyone over one hundred pounds must have seemed "hefty."

I glanced in the mirror behind my father. There I was, all 175 pounds of me. At the age of twelve, I had become quite a looker. I stood at a mighty five feet two inches tall, had thousands of dollars' worth of orthodontia in my mouth, and a cowlick. This was, of course, before I discovered the beauty of hair product. As I stood there staring at the mirror, I wondered what my father could have been thinking.

"You think I am fat?" I asked.

"No, no, no," he said, nearly choking on his words. "Not *fat*... hefty. You could stand to lose a few."

"Well, you know my schedule is so crazy right now," I said. At age twelve, I had already mastered the art of stretching the truth to benefit myself. In my mind, I was the busiest middle schooler on the East Coast. Every morning, I would wake up, go to school, and then come home. That's where my day really began. I would pop *The Sound of Music* into the VCR player and watch one of the most glorious movies ever made while baking a pan of brownies, which I would then eat while scrubbing every inch of my mother's house. I have no idea why as a twelve-year-old I was such a clean freak, but looking back, it certainly explains why I am currently so very OCD. After eating a pan of brownies, I would then recite all of the words Julie Andrews sang to Christopher Plummer after they got married. I so wanted to be her, because what adolescent boy doesn't want to sing to Christopher Plummer? He was such a dreamboat and I totally would have made an amazing stepmother to all of his children. I dreamed of the amazing sing-alongs we would have while fleeing the impending Nazi invasion. All of this was very time-consuming and there was no possible way to fit a new diet into the mix.

"Just change some of your eating habits," my father said. There was no way eating a pan of brownies every day after school was going anywhere. He was delusional. If I didn't eat a pan of brownies and watch *The Sound of Music* every day after school, what the hell was I supposed to do? Exercise? If it hadn't been eleven in the morning, I would have thought he was drunk.

"I don't know, Dad. I am pretty content with the way things are now," I replied. "I've got a pretty good thing going, if ya know what I mean." I winked at him, which he did not find charming in the least. He rolled his eyes and walked out of the room. I sat down on our living room sofa and glanced at the picture of all his children that was sitting on the mantel. Of all his five children, I was definitely the fattest.

My older brother, Tony, was skin and bones. My father would proudly call him "Bones." He certainly didn't have a problem with food. Then there were my sisters, Kim and Jamie. Kim was a superstar soccer player and worked out so much that she could pretty much eat whatever she wanted. It came as no surprise some years later when she revealed she was a lesbian. Jamie, on the other hand, had her cheerleading, and I guess it must have been all of the hurkies, but the girl pretty much kept her weight in check. My younger brother, Kevin, who was a troublemaker, was also really skinny. I guess starting fires in the woods and getting detention every other day speeds up one's metabolism. Then there was my fat ass in the middle of a sea of perfectly toned bodies. Maybe my father was right. Maybe I did need to change my eating habits.

"Your stepmother had an idea just now," my father said as he reentered the room. I looked into his eyes. He was desperate for a perfect family. Had he not been twice divorced at this point he may have gotten one, but he knew what the next best thing would be: the perfect-looking family. "We are going to pay you fifty dollars for every ten pounds you lose."

I think any normal person would have been offended by this, but the Jew in me was just about to blossom and I was going to take up any potential moneymaking opportunity that presented itself.

"It will be really good for you. Isn't your stepmother just the greatest?" my father asked. I highly doubt that Julie Andrews told Kurt Von Trapp that if he held off on the Ho Hos while they were trekking up the Austrian Alps that Ulysses S. Grant would be waiting for him on the other side. She certainly wasn't winning stepmother of the year in my book.

"I'll try it," I said. And so I put my rolling pin away as I began my first-ever diet.

"Nowhere in this diet plan are baked goods listed," I said, looking over a pamphlet I had picked up at the school counselor's office, while sitting at my mother's kitchen table.

"Why are you going on a diet?" my mother asked as she prepared dinner.

"I could stand to lose a couple," I replied. There was no way I could tell her that my father was basically paying me to lose weight. She would have put the kibosh on that immediately, and I had my eye on a ceramic Cinderella figurine that had just come in stock at the Disney store. I had a huge collection of ceramic Disney figurines and my first fifty was going to be spent on the illusive Cinderella that had just come back into stock for a limited time only. I had to have it.

"Okay," my mother said. "We can go on walks together when I get home from work."

"Uh, that's when I am usually watching *The Sound of Music*."

My mother, who should have just thrown me a gay pride parade right then and there just smiled and asked, "What about swimming?"

My cousin Jeri had tried to teach me how to swim the summer before, but I was more of a sit-on-the-sundeck-and-tan-while-drinking-virgin-piña-coladas kind of twelve-year-old.

I winced.

"What about biking?" my mother asked.

"Seems like a lot of work," I replied. "I think I am just going to eat cereal with skim milk for every meal and see if I lose weight. Those bitches on the commercials say that works."

Dieting seemed like such a pain in the ass. I retreated to my room to see if I could afford liposuction, but I was pretty sure twenty-five dollars in quarters wasn't going to do it. Then I came up with an even better plan. I would go to the doctor and tell him to write me a prescription for diet pills, which I would then make my mother pay for, and then weasel a fifty out of my father after I had lost the weight. It was the perfect plan.

A few weeks later, my mother took me to Dr. Waldorf's office. Dr. Waldorf had been my doctor since I was born and bore a striking resemblance to Ronald Reagan. He was about four hundred years old and had always been there for me. I knew he would prescribe diet pills if I just presented a good enough case.

"Why are we here again?" my mother asked as we sat in the waiting room.

"Well, Mother, I read in *Good Housekeeping* that before one starts a diet, one must check to see if everything is where it should be," I replied smartly.

"When the hell did you start reading *Good Housekeeping*?" my mother asked.

I don't know how it happened, but I realized that I was

slowly turning into a pathological liar. My mother knew better than to think I read *Good Housekeeping*. She knew the only thing I read was the *Soap Opera Digest* in the checkout line at the grocery store because I was too cheap to buy the damn thing. I needed to get my hands on these diet pills or else I would never lose weight.

"I don't know, Mother," I said. "Probably the last time I went to the grocery store to buy vegetable oil for my brownies."

God love that woman, she always believed my madcap tales.

The doctor came out and greeted my mother and me. "DR. WALDORF!" my mother yelled with glee as she walked over to help him into the waiting room, "It's so nice to see you . . ."

"Alive," I said under my breath as my mother shot me a dirty look that could have killed.

"Lovely to see you too, darling," Dr. Waldorf said. "How is your husband?"

"We're divorced," my mother said, "and we have been for three years. He's remarried, remember?"

The doctor furrowed his brow and tried his hardest to remember that my mother had told him that she had gotten a divorce. She had done this nearly six times since the actual divorce had taken place. I could tell that the good doctor was losing his shit. Now was the time to hit him with my request.

"Oh yes," Dr. Waldorf replied, "of course, now I remember." He didn't. "What brings you in today?" he asked.

"Just a checkup," I replied. "I want to make sure everything is in order before I start my new diet."

Dr. Waldorf gestured me into his office and I sat on the cold counter while he poked and prodded me. I knew everything was where it needed to be, but I also knew I needed to lose about forty pounds and was too lazy to get off my ass to do anything about it.

"Everything looks in order," Dr. Waldorf said as he removed his stethoscope from my ear. Why he needed to do any of this in order for me to get what I needed was beyond me.

"Hmmm..." I said, "are you sure about that?"

"Of course," he replied, "you are a perfectly healthy twelve-year-old."

Really? I thought. Everyone around me seemed to think that I was overweight, and yet the old doctor seemed to think my weight wasn't a problem.

"Don't you think I am a little bit...overweight?" I asked, fishing.

"Yes," he replied, "but once you hit your growth spurt, you will drop those unwanted pounds before you know it."

I couldn't possibly wait for that to happen. It could take years and that Cinderella figurine wasn't going to buy itself.

"My aunt told me that fen-phen worked for her," I said. Fen-phen was a very popular diet pill at the time that a certain cousin of mine had used to lose about a hundred pounds. The only side effect of the drug was the fact that it caused severe heart attacks, which I was certainly willing to overlook if I made some extra cash in the process.

"You can't be serious," Dr. Waldorf said.

"Uh," I gave him my cute "I-didn't-do-it" half-smile. "Actually."

"Mark," he said, "I cannot, in good conscience, write a prescription for diet pills for a twelve-year-old. I would lose my medical license."

"Really?" I asked. "You can't make this one exception?"

"No." The old man was about to either fall asleep or die,

and looked me in the eyes and replied, "Mark, all you have to do is change your eating habits and exercise a bit. It won't take you very long at all to lose the weight. You're only twelve years old."

Damn it! This wasn't going to be as easy as I had hoped. I was actually going to have to do something to change my appearance. Dr. Waldorf walked me into the waiting room, where my mother had been patiently waiting for me.

"Everything okay?" she asked.

"Yep," the doctor said as he winked at me and nearly fell over. "Mark is fine and ready to start a new diet, isn't that right, Mark?"

"Sure," I said as I grabbed my jacket and left the doctor's office.

The next day, I decided that I was going to have to actually start a diet. I was very concerned because that happened to be the day that I was going to begin the second phase of my Julie Andrews movie marathon with *Mary Poppins,* but important things such as that were going to have to be postponed. I was dieting now. I packed my lunch that day after eating a sensible breakfast of Special K and a banana. It was the first time I had eaten fruit since fat camp. Apparently, fruit snacks are not classified in the fruit food group, which had caused major issues in my dietary plan. I went through my day starving and knew that only an apple was waiting for me when I got home, in lieu of a pan of brownies. Instead of Julie Andrews, an hour-long walk lay ahead. I tried my damndest to get detention that day so I would not have to go home, but my school-time shenanigans were old hat to the teachers by then so I was sent home.

I popped the Julie Andrews Broadway cast recording of *My Fair Lady* into my portable cassette player and began my hour-long walk. I discovered that moving around after a long day of sitting on your ass isn't a half-bad idea. I walked around the neighborhood and when I got home, I felt rejuvenated. So this was exercising? It wasn't as bad as I thought it would be. In fact, I felt amazing. Perhaps this was the beginning of the new and improved Mark Rosenberg.

The school year was coming to an end and I was so happy that I was not going to have to pretend to like any of the people in my middle school anymore. I could be a loner in the summer, go on my walks, eat my healthy meals, and watch movie musicals all afternoon. High school was right around the corner, and I was hell-bent on making a whole new set of friends upon moving on. After a few weeks of dieting, I had my first weigh-in. I had gone from a hefty 175 to a less-hefty 160 in a matter of weeks. Not only had I made my first fifty dollars, I was also halfway to my second. I was such an entrepreneur.

"DAD!" I yelled as I walked into his house that afternoon. "I lost my first ten pounds. Give me fifty bucks!"

"Wow, buddy!" he said. "You look great."

My father had taken my whore of a stepmother on vacation to Tahiti or Tibet or something and had been gone for weeks. He could tell upon his return that I meant business as far as this whole weight-loss project was concerned and was ready to complete his picture-perfect family.

"Let's weigh in, and then you can take me to the mall. I have to hit up the Disney store before July 31 or else I am going to miss Cinderella. We simply cannot have that now, can we?"

"I can't take you to the mall right now, Mark. Your stepmother and I are having a dinner party tonight and we have to prepare. Her family is coming over for Sabbath."

"Seriously?" I replied. Not only did I hate my stepmother, but her family left much to be desired. Her sister and brother-in-law lived on a nudist retreat (but made sure to cover up their junk upon entering our home) and talking to their kids was about as fun as watching ice melt. "Goddamn it, Dad!" I said as I ran up to my room and pouted. I knew that a long night with a bunch of people I did not like talking about a bunch of shit that I did not understand was ahead.

Sabbath rolled around and we all sat at the table to eat dinner. My idiotic stepmother was not the best in the kitchen, and let's just say her food did not dance on one's taste buds. So there was no need for me to cheat tonight. She had made a huge pot of gefilte fish, which is the nastiest-tasting food in the world. I am not exactly sure what goes into gefilte fish, but it seems as though it's just miscellaneous parts of different fish mashed up into a ball of grossness. As the pot was passed, I gracefully declined the soupy fish, but my stepmother stopped me.

"Why don't you eat the gefilte fish, Mark?" she asked.

"Honestly," I replied, "it smells like dead-baby soup."

"MARK!" my father yelled.

"Eat it, Mark!" my stepmother said.

Wait a second. Were these the same people who were paying me to lose weight? I quickly wondered if Stacey had in fact used six to eight dead babies in order to make this soup. The smell was revolting.

"The soup isn't made of dead babies," Stacey said.

"Regardless," I replied. "Moral of the story—not eating it."

My stepmother, whose main goal in life was to make everyone as miserable as possible, smirked.

"I'll pay you fifty dollars to eat the gefilte fish," she replied.

"When did this family start throwing fifties around like Rockefellers?" I asked. "Aren't you paying me fifty dollars to lose weight? Now you want me to eat? Sounds a little ridiculous on your part, doesn't it?"

"Come on, Mark, I will give you fifty bucks right now," she said.

I may not have been a Jew who liked stinky fish, but I was a Jew who liked money and my stepmother knew it. I took some of the fish and put it on my plate. As I lifted my fork to my mouth I said: "I would just like to state for the record, that you people are quite possibly the biggest hypocrites in the world. The only reason I am eating this nasty fish is in fact for the money, because the way you people are spending money on vacations, I am going to have to start a college fund ASAP before all of this family's money is gone." I needed that money and even though I was dieting, a little soup wasn't going to kill me. If anything, it would make me so nauseous that it may be a nice segue into bulimia and I could go back to sitting around on my ass all the time.

I put the spoon with the nasty soup to my nose to smell it. It smelled like crotch rot and looked like the soup in cartoons that has boots floating in it. I hunkered down, bit the bullet, and took a bite. I savored the fishy taste and swallowed. Perhaps it was the fact that I had not eaten any solid food other than Special K in the last two months or the fact that I had never been hungrier in my life, but I ate the soup like it was my job. My father and stepmother looked at me in awe. They should have known better than to make a bet like that with me. Because when you bet the fat kid to eat something, odds are you're losing money on that one.

"Done," I proudly said. "Where's my fifty?"

"Damn it!" my stepmother said under her breath as she stood and got her pocketbook.

I win again, I thought.

"Your stepmother is a whore, and with her recent mental breaks, possibly schizophrenic as well," my mother said the next day. "I don't understand why she would pay you fifty dollars to eat that nasty shit."

"Whatever," I said. "Fifty dollars closer to getting the hell out of here."

"Mark!" my mother said, "watch your fucking language." She paused. "Your father really needs to find something better to do with his time. If he continues paying his children to eat things, going on vacation all of the time, and neglecting everyone, he's going to be a very unhappy camper once Stacey goes off the deep end and actually goes through with killing herself. He needs to get his shit together."

"Yes," I said, "yes, he does." And he still does, God love him.

"On a totally unrelated topic, you've never looked better, young man," my mom said as she took a good look at me. "You look like you've dropped at least two dress sizes."

"Thanks," I replied.

"All of your new friends in high school are going to be so impressed," she said.

"Yeah, you know, I think my middle school friends are dead weight, really. I was planning on getting rid of them anyway, when I got my new bod."

Over the summer I lost over twenty pounds, and when I breezed onto my high school campus for the first time heads were, shall we say, turning. People who had never spoken a word to me were paying attention to me. I had a cool $150 in my pocket and I was four years away from getting the hell out of Maryland. I felt fabulous, like a new person. I was obviously going home after school to watch *Victor Victoria,* but I looked different, and after all, that was the point.

My first day back was amazing. I made new friends and felt fabulous. That is until the end of the day. I saw my friend Jessie, whom I had planned on never speaking to again now that I was hot, but she approached me so I attempted to be polite. She was fat, annoying, and noisy, and the new Mark had no time for any of the above. Her claim to fame was that she had "skinny ankles." The rest of her may have been Herculean, but she prided herself on that fact that she had skinny ankles. As if anyone could see them under all that fat.

"Hey, Mark," Jessie said.

"Yo." I was so cool and skinny now.

"Everyone is talking about your weight loss. You look so great."

"Thanks, Jessie. Maybe I can give you some pointers on how to lose weight." She looked at me and lifted her pants to reveal her "skinny ankles." "Oh, right," I said. "You've got that skinny-ankle thing going for you. Work with it, it's hot." What a cow.

"Yes, everyone is talking about the new and improved Mark," she said.

"That's great. I feel great."

"Yeah," she said with a smirk, "everyone is saying you took laxatives to lose weight over the summer and that's why you are so skinny."

"What?" I was so confused. "What are you talking about?"

"Yeah, Angie told me that's how you lost so much weight."

"First of all," I said, "anyone who knows me knows that I don't need laxatives to shit. My irritable bowel syndrome takes care of that just fine for me, thank you very much. Second, you're a fat cow and a big mouth, Jessie. There is no doubt in my mind that your fat ass started that rumor because you had nothing better to do."

"I am just telling you what I heard," she replied.

"FAT-ASS!" I yelled. Not only was Jessie a big-mouthed cow, but a few months later, she revealed that she was a lesbian, thus providing me with tons of ammo on her for the remaining years of high school.

I ran out of the school wondering what made me think I would ever be popular. I went home and sat on my couch and watched a mini-marathon of Julie, but even she could not make me feel better. I knew what I had to do. I ran to the grocery store and went right to the baking aisle. I was hell-bent on eating every brownie in sight, but then I stopped dead in my tracks.

What am I doing? I thought. *I have lost all of this weight and feel great. Why am I going to waste it all now?*

I paced the supermarket wondering what to do and wandered into the diet aisle. I thought about how fat Jessie was and what she had said to me. I could not believe that everyone thought that I was taking laxatives, when diet and exercise were the cure for what ailed my fatness. I picked up a box of laxatives and looked at the writing on it. How could anyone think that I was taking laxatives? What a preposterous idea.

Then I got an idea. Everyone thought I was taking laxatives already, so what difference would it make if I just started taking them? Before I knew it, I was at the checkout and instead of a box of brownies, I was buying a box of laxatives and the latest copy of *Redbook*. Since everyone thought I was on the diet pills already, I figured I'd buy them, lose more weight, and weasel more money out of my father. Essentially, I was just speeding up the process. That's capitalism at work for you. Over the course of the next two months, I lost twenty more pounds and made one hundred dollars and homecoming court.

BLOW-JOB BETTY

With a new lease on life and a much skinnier facade, our heroine continued through high school, thinking his food issues had come to an end. How wrong he was. Now it was the people around him who had Mark not only questioning his ability to be accepted by his peers, but also wondering: What the fuck is so great about Chili's?

I't's hard trying to fit in in high school. Especially when you're as gay as I was. Prancing around the hallways of your high school singing a medley of songs from the George M. Cohan songbook doesn't really attract best friendships. Most people take the easy route when trying to make friends: sports. For one reason or another our culture embraces those who excel athletically, not realizing that those people usually fall behind in academics and end up fat and not going to college. White boys may be good at basketball when they're in a high school filled with white people, but odds are two hundred to one that there will always be a black kid who will be one hundred times better once they get to college. Then, with their dreams crushed, they retreat to the couch with their six-packs of beer and large pizzas only to pack on the pounds, ending up with shit for brains and grossly overweight. I knew all of these things in high school and didn't bother playing sports at all. I ran track for a bit but was subsequently kicked off the track team after I was caught smoking on school property. I didn't care because to this day I will take a good Marlboro Light over a four-mile hike in the woods. I had to find something to occupy my time, and that something was theater. I was so gay.

Meanwhile, I lived on the cusp of the school district, so the only bus that could pick me up to go to school every morning was the short bus they used for handicapped children, which didn't help me win Most Popular Student at Gaithersburg High.

When I was in eleventh grade, I hated everyone. I had a few close friends, but for the most part, I didn't have time for the stupid high school bullshit that everyone else relished. Cliques, parties, and team sports were not on my radar. I was more concerned with what Erica Kane was wearing that afternoon and a bright young upstart whose career was just beginning to blossom: Britney Spears. Needless to say I had few friends and the fact that I rode the short bus to school every morning didn't help things. The friends I did have, however, were an interesting bunch of people.

I started smoking weed around eleventh grade. Everyone had told me that smoking pot was fun so I tried it, and I became an overnight pothead. It was a nice segue into the other drugs I would become addicted to in college and my raging alcoholism. I had a close group of pothead friends I loved. They included

Maureen, a dear friend to this day; Angie, a skinny dumb slut who slept with everyone; Justin, my one straight male friend in high school; and Betty. Betty was an interesting character. She was heavier, always had braces (I had known the girl for about six years and she always had braces in her mouth), and was a total hippie. Back in high school, I loved hippies. This was of course before I realized they were all lazy pieces of shit who needed to get jobs. Betty was always there to drive us around town when we were supposed to be in school so we could smoke weed during class and not get caught. Betty was also infamous for other things.

Throughout middle school and into high school, I was also friends with Buck Rose. He was a tall, gangly character who had ridiculously curly hair and always sat next to me in class because his last name was Rose and mine was Rosenberg. Buck and I were pretty good friends, so I was completely surprised when Buck rolled into history class one day and told me that he and Betty were now an item.

"You're kidding me," I said.

"Nope," Buck replied. "Betty and I are dating," he said. "Well . . . not so much dating as . . ."

"As . . . what?" I asked.

"Well . . ." Buck said as he leaned toward me as if he were about to tell me some huge secret. "Betty gives me head every weekend in the back of my car after I take her to dinner at Chili's."

"Head?" I asked. I wasn't sure if they were butting heads with each other in the backseat of Buck's car or what.

"You know," Buck said, "blow jobs."

"Wow!" I said. I had never gotten a blow job. I certainly

knew when I did get a blow job that I did not want to get one from someone who had a vagina.

"She's amazing at it," Buck said.

"Really?"

The only time I had seen anyone give a blow job was the rare occasions when no one was in my home and I could download gay porn onto my mother's computer without anyone catching me. I could not believe that such antics were taking place in my very own high school. I really should have known better, since three dumb bitches had gotten knocked up earlier that year and Lord knows there was no immaculate conception involved. Everyone had been getting some but me.

After class, I quickly found Maureen to consult with her about my latest findings.

"Maureen, did you know that Betty gives Buck blow jobs every Saturday night behind the Chili's?" I asked.

"Duh!" she replied. "Betty gives everyone blow jobs behind the Chili's. It's like her claim to fame."

"Really?" Had I been living under a rock for the last three years?

"Yeah," Maureen said. "Jeff, Curtis, Brian, Michael, Cameron, Bill, Ted . . ." The list went on and on. "She's, like, known for it, you know?"

"No, I did not know, but I am glad I found this out when I did."

"Why?" Maureen asked.

"I don't know," I said. I really wanted to get a blow job, but knew I did not like girls. I was really more curious about what it felt like. I had obviously not come out of the closet, but considering I did not play sports, was involved in theater, and had a fondness for soap operas and show tunes, it was pretty clear to everyone that I was a huge homo. However, the only other gay kid at our school was this crazy black kid named Darius whom everyone hated and I certainly could not get a blow job from him. Everyone would find out and hate me too. "This is all very interesting. Everyone is getting blow jobs except me."

"It's okay, Mark. You will get a blow job sooner or later."

Fall passed and Betty continued giving Buck his weekly blow job behind the Chili's until January rolled around and I got word from Maureen and Angie that Betty was no longer blowing Buck behind the now-infamous chain restaurant.

"I don't know," Maureen said, "something about Betty asking Buck to go down on her and him refusing to do it."

"What?" I replied. "I thought this was like a barter system. Betty gets free meals at Chili's and Buck gets free blow jobs."

"I guess not," Maureen said.

"Interesting," I said.

"Besides, would you want to go down on Betty?"

The thought repulsed me. I wanted to go down on a girl about as much as I wanted a sandpaper hand job from Marlon Brando circa *The Godfather*. But I couldn't let anyone know about my disgust with vaginas just yet. I had to play it cool.

"I don't know," I said. "Maybe if we went to the salad bar at Ruby Tuesday's or something and I was in the right mood."

"Seriously? She's pretty foul," Maureen said, "and she's given blow jobs to, like, half the school."

"True," I replied. And she was a girl. Nasty.

Shortly after this exchange I found Betty in her car, ready to drive to McDonald's for lunch. I hopped in.

"Hey, Betty," I said.

"What's up, Mark?" she replied.

"Nothing much. I heard that you and Buck aren't going out anymore. I'm sorry to hear that."

"It's okay," she said. "He just wasn't giving me what I wanted."

"So I heard. Listen, I was wondering if you wanted to get dinner this weekend."

"Why not? I am free Saturday night. I guess I will be free every Saturday night from now on."

"Maybe not," I said.

"What do you mean?"

"Well, maybe we could date," I said. I really did not want to date Betty, or any other girl for that matter, but I did want a blow job, so I had to play it cool.

"Really?" she said as her eyes lit up.

"Why not?" I replied. "Let's meet up at the mall on Saturday night. They just opened a new Chevys. We can eat there."

"Perfect."

In high school I discovered the beauty of the tanning salon. I had really bad acne as a teenager and I had read in *Cosmopolitan* that tanning could decrease acne. I was the only teenager at Gaithersburg High School who walked into class every day looking like George Hamilton, and I loved it. Everyone would always ask me if I had taken a trip to an exotic locale the weekend before. I never answered, thinking my peers would think I was cooler than them if I left it to their imagination. But I am sure they knew the only trip I had taken recently was to the Swiss Alps with Julie Andrews and the rest of the crew from *The Sound of Music*.

That Saturday I went to the tanning salon at the mall before meeting Betty. After tanning, I stepped outside and smoked a cigarette as I waited for cancer to come and bitch-slap me from behind. Finally, I saw Betty's car pull up to the Chevys at the mall and greeted her.

"Hey, Betty," I said as she got out of her car. She was such a mess. Her hair was always all over the place and those braces. The thought of kissing her repulsed me, but I really wanted a blow job.

"Mark," she said as she greeted me, "so great to see you." We had just seen each other the previous day at school and had planned on meeting, so I was not exactly sure why seeing me surprised her, but I let it slide. Maybe she thought I wasn't going to show. I wanted that blow job and would risk anything to get it.

We went to Chevys and chatted. Betty told me about her relationship with Buck and how things hadn't worked out. I didn't want to tell her the real reason things didn't work out was because he didn't want to go down on her, but instead I sat and listened intently.

"I really liked Buck," Betty said.

"Yeah, he's a good guy," I replied. "I am not always comfortable with his fashion choices, but he's a good guy."

"Well, we're dating now, so I guess it doesn't matter."

"Right," I said. I couldn't believe I was in a full-blown relationship. We were discussing such adult topics, like her past flings and the rise of Britney Spears on the Billboard charts. Little did we know at the time that Britney would be a full-blown superstar. But how can you predict magic like that happening? You just can't. Anyway, when dinner was over, I walked Betty to her car and we kissed. It was the first time I had kissed a girl and it was kind of slimy. She stuck her tongue down my throat and began wiggling it around. I did the same, except I was pretending Bailey from *Party of Five* was on the receiving end of my kiss. It made it all worth it. However, I was a little miffed that I had taken her to dinner and didn't get my complimentary blow job. Wasn't this how relationships worked? I was confused.

On Monday, I ran in to Buck and told him what had happened.

"BUCKY," I yelled as history class was about to begin.

"What up, Rosie?"

"Nothing," I said pointing to my pants. "Absolutely nothing."

"Uh, what do you mean?"

"I went out with Betty on Saturday night. I took her to Chevys and was expecting a blow job afterward, but got nothing. What the fuck?"

"Mark, Mark, Mark," Buck said. "You have to take her to Chili's."

"What fucking difference does it make?" I asked.

"I don't know," he continued. "Something about that restaurant really turns that girl on."

"Are you serious?"

"Yes. I have taken her to P.F. Chang's, T.G.I. Friday's, Macaroni Grill, you name it. The only time I have gotten a blow job out of that girl is after Chili's."

"Christ!" I replied. Not that I didn't like Chili's, it was just out of the way and not nearly as convenient as, say, the Cheesecake Factory that was right down the street from my house.

"Just take her to Chili's. You'll get your blow job."

The next Saturday came around and Betty and I were off to Chili's. When we got there, Betty ordered almost everything off the menu. Perhaps Buck was right, perhaps this place did get Betty off. We barely spoke throughout the entire meal. I have never seen anyone go down on a sampler platter the way Betty did that night, and I was hoping her feeding frenzy was a preview of what was to come. After dinner was over, Betty and I got into the car and she drove me behind the Chili's and we both hopped into the backseat.

Finally! I thought.

She mauled me. She took my clothes off and went down on me in the backseat of her car in the parking lot behind Chili's. Who knew Chili's was such an aphrodisiac? As she was giving me head, all I could do was picture my beloved Bailey and his dimples. He was so cute, and such a great brother to all of those obnoxious siblings of his. Then I thought of how lucky Jennifer Love Hewitt was that she got to kiss him every week. Besides that pesky alcohol problem of his, Bailey was the perfect man. Then I turned to see Betty bobbing up and down. She was certainly no Scott Wolf, I will tell you that much right now. There was something about her that was so simply unappealing, but I let her continue blowing me until she was done.

"Dessert!" she said after she had finished.

Gross, I thought.

Was I supposed to cuddle with her now? I didn't know what protocol to follow, as this was my first blow job and first girlfriend, so I put my arm around hers.

"You know," Betty said, "my pants are still on."

"They sure are, aren't they?" I replied.

"What should we do about that?"

Chunks of the burrito I just eaten had began to well up in my throat. The thought of going down on Betty was like eating a rotten egg omelet. Neither of which I had any interest in doing.

"I should probably get home," I said.

"Seriously?" she asked.

"Uh, yeah, why?"

"Because my pants are still on."

"Yeah, that seems to be a problem for you, huh?"

"YES!" she yelled.

"Well, you can drive me home pantsless if that helps."

"GODDAMN IT!" she yelled. "I just gave you a blow job. Now give me one."

I didn't know what to do, so I did the only thing that came to mind. I threw up all over Betty.

"GROSS!" she yelled.

Spewing chunks of regurgitated burrito and brownie sundae all over Betty was not nearly as gross as going down on her would have been. She drove me home and we sat in silence the whole way back.

On Monday, I confronted Maureen about whether or not she had heard about what had happened on Saturday night. Since we all had cell phones as we were breezing into the new millennium, she heard about it, seconds after I had gotten out of Betty's car.

"Yeah, Betty told me about what happened. Pretty disgusting on your part," Maureen said.

"I have not felt the same since. I think I may have gotten food poisoning."

"Funny how that kicked in right about the time Betty asked you to go down on her," she replied.

"Right," I said.

"You need to take her out again. Valentine's Day is coming. You should do something nice for her."

Girls, myself included, love Valentine's Day. It's the most romantic day of the year and girls cash in on it like JonBenét's mother at a beauty pageant.

Shortly after Maureen left me, Betty approached.

"Sorry about the other night," I said to her. "I think I must have eaten something that did not agree with me."

"It's okay," she replied. "Valentine's is this weekend. Should we do something special?"

"Sure, what would you like to do?"

"We can go to Chili's."

"Seriously? I don't think I ever want to go back there again."

"I am the girl and you are supposed to do what I want. It's Valentine's for Christ's sake."

"Fine. We can go to Chili's. Pick me up at six," I replied. I don't know what this girl's fascination with Chili's was all about, but I knew it wasn't healthy or normal. Maybe it was the spinach-and-artichoke dip or the never-ending bowl of chips, but the girl literally got off on Chili's. I had no interest in ever eating at Chili's again or dating Betty at this point, but knew I would be a real bastard if I didn't go through with it.

When Valentine's Day rolled around, Betty picked me up and off to Chili's we went. Again, she went crazy with the appetizers. I wondered if she had eaten at all that week. I knew her mother made killer turkey sandwiches and wondered why she was so hungry. I honestly didn't understand what this girl's deal was. Blow jobs don't really increase one's appetite that much, so I questioned her motives.

After the feeding frenzy, Betty drove behind the Chili's and parked in the lot behind the restaurant. I knew what came next: another blow job. I was excited that I would now have two under my belt, but all I could think about while she was giving me head, besides Bailey Salinger, was the inevitable question of whether or not I was going to blow her afterward. As if the girl had a penis.

After she was done, she made another comment about dessert and I almost lost it again, but kept it to myself.

"Ha," I said. I would have preferred a blondie, but I guess she liked blow jobs to top her meals off.

"So . . ." she said, "what do you want to do now?"

"Nap," I said jokingly, "or just flat-out go to bed. I am pooped."

"I mean, what do you want to do with me?" she asked.

"I don't know . . . take you home?" I knew her game and I wasn't playing it. "I am really wiped out."

"MARK!" she yelled. "Take my pants off!"

"Uh, I don't think I am really comfortable with that. Remember what happened last time?"

"Go down on me!"

Suddenly I felt like Tori Spelling in every Lifetime movie ever. Was I about to get date-raped?

"Betty, I don't think I can," I replied.

"I know you can, so just do it!"

"No, I don't think I can. And I don't think I can date you anymore either."

"Seriously? You're breaking up with me on Valentine's Day?"

Shit! I had totally forgotten it was still Valentine's Day. Now I really was going to look like a bastard.

"Betty, I just don't think this is going to work out. I don't think I can afford to take you to Chili's every weekend and your pressuring me to eat you out is clearly not agreeing with my digestive system."

"God, why does this always happen?"

The reason that this always happened could be the fact that vagina is disgusting, but I decided to refrain from telling her that.

"I'm sorry, Betty," I said as I got into the front seat of her car.

That was the last time I ever ate at Chili's. Besides the fact that I had thrown up all over someone who was basically prostituting herself out for chicken wings, something about this entire situation left a bad taste in my mouth.

SEXY PANTS

After graduating high school and moving to New York to go to college, our fearless heroine realized that you can always go home. And what happens when you go home? You're thrown back into the bullshit that makes you realize why you left in the first place. After three years of living in New York that consisted of Mark coming out of the closet (shocker!), perfecting the art of being a functional alcoholic, and becoming Manhattan's favorite party boy, Mark begins to question his family's real motives and finds a name for what he's spent his life doing.

On Thanksgiving, junior year of college, I breezed into D.C. to visit the family. Every time I came home to see them for a holiday, I felt the need to get as hammered as possible the evening before. This prepared me to deal with a night of inevitable dramatic revelations and the subsequent screaming and door slamming that followed. My childhood education of soap operas prepared me for drama surrounding special events, because a holiday with your family that doesn't involve misery or the surprise revelation of a "secret family" is like a cake without icing—incomplete. In order to detour myself from the dramatics, I would get blackout drunk the evening before, which would in turn lead to more dramatics. Luckily, that's all in the past, but I can always rely on the rest of my family to provide the hysterics in my sobriety.

The night before this particular Thanksgiving, like any normal family, I met up with my sister Jamie at a gay bar in downtown D.C. We had a couple of cocktails and both commiserated about the fact that we were still single. For one reason or another, Jamie is like a magnet for gay men: They love her. It's probably because she lives in D.C.'s gayborhood, is drop-dead gorgeous, and is always dressed in the hottest fashions she can afford. I got up to refill our drinks and when I returned Jamie was surrounded by a group of gay men. Bitch was holding court and all of them were hanging on her every word.

"MARK!" she yelled. "Look at all of these fabulous men I just met." Suddenly Jamie was like Madonna, surrounded by ten to twelve men who looked like they could have been her backup dancers.

"Hello," I said as I handed my sister her cocktail. I introduced myself to all of Jamie's new gay friends. Shortly thereafter, Jamie and I were left with just Chuck and Skip, a couple that was clinging to her every word. Considering most gay guys have the attention spans of four-year-old girls, I found it quite interesting that these two were still schmoozing with her. When they had gotten up to refresh their drinks, my sister leaned over to speak to me.

"Skip and Chuck want to have a threesome with you," she said.

"What?" I said.

"Hello deaf-o! Skip and Chuck want to have a threesome with you."

"Wait . . . what?" I said. "Are you trying to liaise a three-way for your little brother?"

"Why not?"

"I'm not really comfortable with all of this," I replied. Skip, for one, looked like he had been kicked in the face repeatedly as a child, and Chuck looked and acted as if his mother drank throughout her pregnancy with him. If I were to have a three-way, it certainly wouldn't be with this dynamic duo.

"Come on, Mark, it will be fun," my sister said.

"Jamie, what the hell is your problem?" I asked. I didn't need an answer. She was hammered. Why else would she have cared?

I excused myself and went to the upstairs part of the bar. I didn't want to tell my sister, but I was still a virgin . . . well, an ass virgin at least. I had dated my first boyfriend, Sebastian, for some time but we never went all the way. He was scared because at the age of thirty, he had never had sex. One time, in an attempt to loosen him up, we bought three dildos in the hopes that we would finally be able to have sex like adults. A big one, a medium-size one, and a small one—just to test the waters. Trying to keep the mood light, I decided to name the dildos. The biggest one was Angela Channing, the matriarch on *Falcon Crest*. She always meant business, so I figured she was the obvious name for the biggest dildo. The middle-size one was Maggie Channing. She was pleasant to be around, but if you pissed her off, she would go bat-shit crazy on a bitch. The smallest one I called Lance Cumson. He was Angela's grandson and basically did whatever she told him to.

I've found that plastic penises are more fun when you name them after characters on 1980s primetime soaps. Night after night, Sebastian would attempt to stick these plastic penises up his rear end but he couldn't even get the tip of Lance Cumson inside of him without crying like a little baby. I never understood the need for the whole dildo fiasco in the first place. For one thing, we both had penises of our own, and for another, Sebastian was pushing thirty. Not having sex at that point is a little ridiculous. Moral of the story is, at twenty years old, I was still a card-carrying member of the V-Club. I didn't know a ton about sex, but I did know that I wasn't going give it up to Skip and/or Chuck.

I lingered around the upstairs portion of the bar. All I could see were hammered gay guys pairing off left and right in hopes to extend the evening a little longer, because we all knew tomorrow was to be spent with the family. The bar that night smelled like every gay bar I've ever been to: alcoholism and regret. After a while, I spotted a very good-looking guy across the way. He was tall and had long blond hair and blue eyes. He walked over to say hello.

"Hi, I'm Mickey," he said.

"Mark," I replied.

"What are you doing here, all alone on the night before Thanksgiving?" he asked.

"I'm with my sister," I replied. "She's downstairs. God only knows what she's up to now."

I had downed about four cocktails and was feeling pretty good. Before I knew it, Mickey and I were pounding drinks and I was hammy hammed. I was almost to the point of being "date-rape drugged" wasted, but I wasn't quite there yet. Mickey and I drank and laughed and before I knew it, I was flirting with not only a blond but a blackout as well. As I continued drinking, my sister sashayed upstairs.

"Way to go, Mark," she said. "Chuck and Skip left. I guess you're not going to have that threesome after all."

"You're really in it to win it with this whole threesome business, huh?" I asked.

"Mickey?" my sister said, turning her attention to my new friend.

"Oh my God, Jamie Rosenberg! How the hell have you been?"

Suddenly, I was out and Jamie was in. All attention was on my sister. I stood there while the two of them caught up. Apparently my sister had become the empress of gay D.C. while I was away at school. After they finished, my sister leaned in and whispered in my ear: "You should sleep with him. He's good people. He totally saved my ass at JCC summer camp."

With that, my sister left me with Mickey to fend for myself. She told me that I needed to have sex with him and that she would pick me up the next morning and drive me to my mother's.

We went back to Mickey's apartment on M Street. Before I knew it we were making out like teenagers. As if on cue, a few minutes into it, Mickey pulled out a small Baggie and rolled-up a twenty-dollar bill and asked me if I wanted to do coke. It was already three in the morning and I knew I had to sit through Thanksgiving dinner the next day. Could I potentially do this while coming off of cocaine? I concluded that yes, I could, and proceeded to snort cocaine and make out with Mickey until five in the morning.

The next day, Jamie picked me up from Mickey's and drove me to my mother's.

"So . . ." she asked.

"So, what?" I replied. I was cracked out from the drugs I had done the night before and less than three hours of sleep I had gotten.

"Did you guys do it?"

"Jamie." I paused. "I'm still technically a virgin and not really sure I'm ready to give it up," I said. My sister looked shocked. Either that or she was severely hung over. I honestly don't recall. I continued, "And since when did you become so invested in my sex life?"

"I don't know," she said. "I went on six J-Dates last week and haven't heard back from any of them. This is really all I've got going on this weekend, if I'm being honest." Little did we know that at this time a year from now, she would be knocked up.

Jamie dropped me off at my mother's house and she greeted me.

"Mark!" my mother said, "you look so . . . skinny."

"I know," I said as I hugged her. "I lost the baby weight."

"Baby fat," she replied.

"Baby weight," I repeated.

"Shut the fuck up and get in here!"

I had lost a few pounds during junior year of college. Keeping up with the Joneses and substituting food with booze and drugs will really help to shed those excess inches. However, whenever I came home for any occasion, I gorged like one of Sally Struthers's children-in-need after a forty-mile trek through the African Sahara. For me, coming home meant eating like I had ten assholes. I guess being around my family made me feel like a fat kid again and I would just go ahead and embrace it.

That Thanksgiving, I inhaled food like someone had told me that I had a meeting with a firing squad the next morning. My mother looked on in awe. Rumors of bulimia spread like wildfire that holiday season. No one could believe that I ate as much as I had. What they didn't know was that doing a ton of cocaine the night before speeds up one's metabolism the next day. Cocaine makes you so hungry that you would literally eat dead baby if someone served it to you on a garnished plate. That evening Mickey called me and asked if I wanted to come over. Having met my quota of family time, I agreed. When I arrived, we started making out and he once again offered me drugs.

"I'm not one hundred percent sure what this is," Mickey said.

"What do you mean?" I asked. "Isn't it coke?"

"I don't know. My friend Patrick gave it to me. He said he thought it may be heroin."

"Well, try it out and let me know what you think it is. If you start having convulsions on the floor, I'll know not to touch it."

"Wouldn't you take me to the hospital if I was having convulsions?" Mickey asked.

I thought about it for about a minute and replied: "Of course."

Mickey did a bump of the mysterious substance while I waited. I stared at him to see if he was going to die or pass out, and when he hadn't five minutes later, I did a bump as well. I'm still not sure what was in that bag, but that night I got the most fucked up I had ever been in my life. Mickey and I sat around and talked about stupid shit and watched reruns of *Dynasty*. We continued chatting and before I knew it, Mickey and I were naked and about to have sex.

"I'm a virgin," I told him.

"That's okay, I'll be gentle."

That night, high on a mysterious substance that may or may not have been heroin, I lost my virginity. It wasn't as bad as I thought it was going to be. It was certainly a hell of a lot better than having Lorenzo Lamas up my ass.

The next morning when I woke up, I was starving. I briefly wondered if I could have been pregnant. I had skipped most of health class in middle school, so at the age of twenty, I still believed there may have been a way for me to get impregnated. I told Mickey that the least he could do after stealing my virginity in the night was to take me out to breakfast. I do not think that he imagined it would be a ninety-dollar affair.

We sat down and I immediately ordered three eggs, bacon, toast, two waffles, and a cup of coffee with an iced tea chaser.

"I'll have yogurt," Mickey told the waitress.

"Yogurt?" I said. "Seriously?" I gave him a dirty look for making me feel like a fat-ass.

We chatted until our food arrived. Then all conversation stopped. I shoveled food into my mouth as if I had never eaten before. It was very reminiscent of when I was young and fat and would take three-mile walks every day to stay in shape. I was, however, taking those three-mile walks to Burger King and would proceed to scarf two Whoppers and walk back home, thus defeating the purpose of walking three miles in the first place. Mickey looked at me with awe.

"When's the last time you ate?" he asked.

"Yesterday, why?" I replied.

"Because you're eating like—" he stopped.

I stopped eating and looked up at him with crumbs around my mouth.

"You're eating like you're eating your feelings," he said.

"What?"

"You're eating your feelings."

"Come again?"

"Are you okay with this whole lost-virginity thing?" he said.

Quite honestly, the only thing on my mind was the plate of food in front of me.

"What do you mean eating my feelings?"

"You know, when you're upset about something and you binge-eat to forget about it."

Finally, someone had given a proper name to what I had been doing for years.

"I'm not upset about anything," I replied.

"Okay, I just wanted to check."

I continued eating, and when I was finished, I ate the rest of Mickey's yogurt. I was starving. Perhaps whatever drugs were served the previous night had baby laxatives in them. After breakfast, Mickey dropped me off at my mother's.

Since Mickey lived in D.C. and I lived in New York, we both knew there was no potential to have a worthwhile relationship. Because of geographical issues, we decided whenever we were horny, we would text-message each other the words *sexy pants,* which was code for "I'm ready to have phone sex." That, ladies and gentlemen, is what I like to call communicating like adults.

It is tradition in my family after gorging on Thanksgiving dinner to go out for pizza the next night. As if we hadn't eaten enough already. I ate about four hundred slices of pizza that evening. I remembered what Mickey had said. Perhaps I was more upset about this whole lost-virginity situation than I thought I was. As I was gorging food, my other sister, Kim, asked, "Are you coming down off of something?"

"I'm not sure," I replied. The ingredients of the powder I

had snorted the night before were still unknown to me and I wasn't sure what was going on. I was also still pretty sure I had gotten pregnant.

"Are you okay?" Kim asked.

"I think so."

"What's going on?"

"I lost my virginity last night," I said.

"WHAT?!" she yelled.

Everyone looked up to see what my sister was yelling about and she shrugged it off.

"You were still a virgin until last night?" she asked.

"Well, I've hooked up before. I mean, I'd done everything but..."

"But, butt?"

"Roger that," I said.

"With who?"

"A guy called Mickey Goldman."

"OH MY GOD!" My sister yelled again.

"What the fuck are you two yelling about down there?" my mother asked.

"Uh, nothing," I replied.

My sister continued: "You know Jamie and I—"

"Yes," I cut her off. "I know. You went to Jewish Community Center summer camp with him. It's a fun Rosenberg family fact that I am now very much aware of, thank you very much."

"Interesting. Does Jamie know about this?"

"Are you kidding me?" I asked. "She orchestrated this whole ordeal."

"Girl needs to get a hobby. Or a boyfriend."

"Cheers to that," I said as we clinked our beer glasses.

I didn't think about Mickey very much. Once I was back

in New York, I didn't have time for *sexy pants* text messages because I had to wrap up finals and get my social calendar in check for the holidays. Besides, he lived in D.C. and I lived in New York—we weren't looking to be in a relationship. As my mother would say, "Two blonds don't make a right." A few weeks later I went back to D.C. for Christmas and stopped at my father's office first. When I got there, my father was in a meeting, so I waited for him in the lobby. I fingered through a *Highlights* magazine and enjoyed the vocal prowess of Dionne Warwick as I waited. My father always had the best music playing in the lobby of his office.

After humming the entire theme from *Valley of the Dolls,* I saw my father approach the lobby with a man who looked like he may or may not have been inside of me weeks earlier.

"MARK!" my father yelled as I got up to greet him. "Do you know Mickey?" he said as Mickey came from behind to shake my hand.

I must have had that look that people get when they find out they're adopted. I was horrified.

"Hello, Mickey," I said as I reached out to shake his hand.

"Mickey has been a client of mine for years. You know kids these days with their terrible driving habits and drugs charges." I looked at Mickey awkwardly and my father continued. "Did you know that he went to JCC summer camp with your sisters?" Mickey gave me a look that said either "I just shit my pants" or "I've never been so embarrassed."

"I did not. I did not know that you went to JCC summer camp with Kim and Jamie. Fascinating," I said.

"He got into a little accident a few months ago and I was just helping him with some paperwork. We've known him for so long, it's almost as if he's like my own son."

Ew. Wait . . . did I have sex with my own brother? With my family, anything is possible.

Mickey and I exchanged pleasantries and he quickly left my father's office.

My father and I then proceed to catch up, and as we were walking out of the office doors I received a text message that read: *sexy pants*!

That was the last time I ever saw Mickey, but I have to thank him for teaching me so many life lessons. He taught me that when presented with an unknown drug, it's probably best to just say no. He taught me that losing your virginity is best saved for strangers because if all doesn't go well, you never have to see them again unless they're clients of your father's. And finally, Mickey had identified my lifelong struggle with food and had given it a name. He explained the essence of what eating my feelings is and I continue to embrace it to this day.

AS THE REVOLVING DOOR
OF DELIVERY MEN TURNS

For years, Mark had been gorging on food alone until he met the one person who shared his love of food to the extent he did. Some would call our heroine's new friend a companion, but Mark calls her his soul mate.

Fall of 2003 was a magical time for everyone. Audiences were delighting in the hilarious genius that was *Bruce Almighty* and America's sweetheart-in-training Kelly Clarkson was amazing the country with her golden vocals. I had the great pleasure of meeting a new friend, Sally. Sally had met my friend Tom while fighting over the price of her head shots at Kinko's. Shortly after, Tom dragged Sally to meet me at the Edison Diner on 47th Street.

"Can I get you three something to drink?" the waitress said as she approached our table.

"I'll have a Diet Coke," I said.

"OH MY GOD!" Sally screamed.

"What is it?" I asked.

"I LOVE Diet Coke," she replied.

It was love at first sight. Not only had we bonded over a mutual love of Diet Coke, she was also a fan of other essentials in my life: musical theater and Britney Spears. I had finally met my intellectual equal.

Another reason I love Sally is because she is one of the most gorgeous people I have ever known—inside and out. On the outside, she has long brown hair, a smile for days, wide eyes, and boobs as big as her heart. She also enjoys the sun, so on any given day it's always a question as to what nationality she really is. On the inside, she's a truck driver. She drinks beer like it's her job, curses like a sailor, and loves all types of sporting events, especially ones that revolve in or around Buffalo, her hometown. You never want to play a game with her either. She is the worst sport ever and a bad loser and turns any game night into a blood sport. She's the greatest person I've ever known. She's extremely sweet to your face but will be the first to tell you to go fuck yourself if you piss her off. She truly is a magical human being.

A few weeks into our friendship, Sally came over to my apartment for a sleepover. We dined on French toast and onion rings and watched Britney's last world tour. I was so happy that I had found someone on my level. But it wasn't until that night that I realized just how on my level Sally really was.

"Uh, I'm so full," I said as I turned out the light to go to bed.

"I know, me too," Sally replied.

As we lay there attempting to go to sleep, Sally rolled over and said: "You know what would have made this night complete?"

"What's that?"

"Brownie sundaes."

"True that!" I replied. "I fucking love brownie sundaes. A warm brownie with vanilla ice cream and whipped cream. Nothing tops that!"

"I know, I kind of want one now," Sally said.

"Well, it's 2 A.M. I think it's a bit late," I said. "Speaking of desserts, I do love a nice black-and-white cookie. I really only like the white part though. Does that make me a racist?"

"*That* is not what makes you a racist."

"Okay, good." I felt relieved.

As I continued trying to doze off, Sally rolled over once more and said: "You know what I really love?"

"What's that?"

"Pigs in a blanket."

"Me too," I replied.

"But not like the microwave pigs in a blanket. I like putting hot dogs in crescent rolls then sticking them in the oven. That's the best."

I was getting excited: "Oh my God, I know! With hot mustard. Delish!"

Mind you, we had eaten all evening long. Yet we continued to speak of food well into the night.

"You know what else I love? Nachos. Next time we have a sleepover, we should make homemade nachos."

"And taco dip!" Sally said with glee. "I make the best fucking taco dip you'll ever have."

"I know! Next time we get together we should just have Night of a Thousand Dips. I can make spinach-and-artichoke dip. And cheese dip. It will be amazing."

"Oh, let's do that next week."

"Sally?" I asked.

"Yes."

"I want Chicken McNuggets. Let's walk across the street to McDonald's and get some."

"Okay."

Sally and I walked across the street from my apartment at 2 A.M. and got two twenty-piece Chicken McNuggets at the twenty-four-hour McDonald's. I loved Sally. You would have thought that the two of us were morbidly obese the way we spoke of food, but we just loved to eat—everything in sight.

A few years after I met Sally, her roommate moved out and she asked me if I wanted to move in with her. Her apartment on the Upper East Side was less of an apartment and more of a youth hostel. There was no living room or common area; there were simply three bedrooms that were connected by a long hallway that led to a small kitchen and an even smaller bathroom. Each bedroom had a loft bed, so there was really no headroom once you got into the bedrooms, so you would have to squat once you entered the room. It was almost paradise, but not quite. When Sally asked me to be her roommate, I jumped at the chance. At first I believed it would be a good idea to move in with Sally because I loved her and the rent was cheaper than what I was paying at the time. I then calculated the amount of money we would most likely spend on groceries and realized I would probably be in the red if I moved in with her, but didn't really care.

"Can you imagine the feeding frenzies we will have?" she asked.

"No," I said with a straight face. "No. I honestly cannot."

Once I moved into the crack shack that was my new apartment, I decided that I was going to have to give my new abode a fitting name.

"Let's call our apartment La Boulaie. Like Dorian's house on *One Life to Live*."

"I don't know what any of those words mean, but it sounds good to me," Sally replied.

Once I got settled, the fun began. Every Saturday night, Sally and I would go out for "Blackout or Back Out Saturday Nights." Meaning every Saturday we would either black out from drinking or if you couldn't take the heat, you would be forced to back out and go home only to be ridiculed the next day by the other party. It was a constant shit show of boozing, debauchery, and late-night hookups. On Sunday, Sally and I would sit on her bed and watch reruns of *Beverly Hills, 90210* hung over all day long.

Being hung over meant being hungry. Drinking can take a lot out of you, and if you find yourself running from the law or an ex, it can also be a really good form of cardio. Every Sunday Sally and I would park it on her bed and a day of eating would commence. We would order at least three meals from delivery in one day. Once we ordered from the same place three times in one day and the deliverymen thought we were high. We weren't—we were just fat pigs.

A few months into our cohabitation, a horrible blizzard struck Manhattan. Sally and I prepared for lockdown.

"Okay," I said, "I'm going to go to the gym real quick, in anticipation of eating my feelings all night. I'll stop at the store on my way home and get everything we need for what I'm sure will be a three-day feeding frenzy."

"Perfect. I'll stay here and watch TV while you're gone. We want to make sure it's warm for your return."

I went to the gym and on my way home went to the store and bought one hundred dollars' worth of groceries. Not one protein, vegetable, or fruit. Nothing nutritious, just junk—the way we liked it. I returned home to find Sally waiting for me. I don't know why I even bothered going to the gym. I think I had gained two pounds just from looking at all of the crap I had just bought at the store.

"You know what I could really go for tonight?" Sally asked.

"What's that?"

"Fried chicken."

"Seriously, Sally?" I asked. "I just spent a hundred bucks at the store and it's starting to snow. I'm not going back out there to get fried chicken. What's with the cravings anyway? What are you, pregnant?"

"NO!" Sally yelled. "I just really want fried chicken."

"I got the essentials. Pigs in a blanket, stuff to make taco dip and brownie sundaes, carrots."

"Carrots?"

I started laughing hysterically. "That was just for us. I'm kidding."

Sally laughed like she had the devil inside of her and replied: "I was about to say? Carrots? What the fuck are we supposed to do with carrots?"

Nothing about this conversation was funny at all, but we laughed for about five more minutes until Sally got serious again.

"What are we going to do about this fried-chicken situation?"

"We have enough food for days, we don't need it," I replied.

"I want fried chicken!"

"Listen, bitch," I said, "if you want fried chicken, you can go down the street to get it. I'm not going out in the snow again."

"I have a better idea. I'll see if KFC delivers."

Sally went into her bedroom as I continued putting the groceries away.

"Fuck, yeah! They do!" she called from the other room. "What do you want?"

"Fried chicken, I guess," I said.

"You guess?" Sally said as if I had just offended her. "They have, like, a menagerie of side dishes to choose from. How can you just 'guess' you want fried chicken? I thought you were in it to win it with this whole feeding-frenzy thing."

"Okay, I'll take a side of mac and cheese and mashed potatoes."

"Now, that's what I'm talking about!"

"Sally?"

"Yes."

"See if there is a Pizza Hut attached to that KFC. We may as well kill two birds with one stone."

"God love you, Mark, for thinking ahead."

Sally then proceeded to order fifty dollars' worth of food from the KFC/Pizza Hut down the street. When the deliveryman arrived after having made the two-block trek in nearly a foot of snow, I tipped him twenty bucks and sent him on his way. Sally and I gorged that weekend like we never had before. It's what I imagine the craft services table would have looked like if Marlon Brando and Dom DeLuise ever teamed up to do a film together. Buckets of chicken, pizza, dips, pigs in a blanket, you name it, we ate it that weekend. But the pièce de résistance was always dessert. That night, we were going to make the brownie sundaes to end all brownie sundaes.

"So," I said to Sally as we entered the kitchen, "we have all of the ingredients. All we need to do is mix it up and put that fucker in the oven."

"Thank God we have these to look forward to," Sally said as if we hadn't eaten enough already that day.

As I was mixing the ingredients into the bowl, I reached up to grab a measuring cup and knocked a glass over and into the bowl, and it shattered into a thousand pieces.

"GODDAMN IT!" I yelled.

"Oh no, now we can't have brownies," Sally cried.

"Why not?"

"Uh, because there are thousands of shards of broken glass in the mix."

"Can't we just pick them out?" I asked.

"Seriously?" Sally said. She looked back at me and realized that I was in fact being 100 percent serious and continued, "No!"

"Motherfucker. I really wanted brownie sundaes."

"Oh well," Sally said. "We have eaten enough today."

"No!"

"What?"

"I'm going back to the store to get another thing of mix."

"But, there are like two feet of snow on the ground right now," Sally said.

"I want brownie sundaes, goddamn it."

"You wouldn't get me fried chicken, but you will go out in two feet of snow to get brownie mix?"

"Yeah," I said.

"Well you can go, but I'm not leaving."

"Fine."

I put on everything I owned and walked out the door. I trudged through two feet of snow and back to the store (which hardly had anything in it, thanks to the mass hysteria caused by the snow) to retrieve brownie mix. When I returned, Sally was sprawled out on her bed with crumbs all over her chest.

"Thank God you're back, I was getting worried," Sally said as she got up.

"It's miserable outside. I never want to leave this apartment again."

We made our brownie sundaes and lay about in our own filth for the next two days. When Monday came, I got up and had a message from my boss telling me that work was optional that day because there had been so much snow. I loved not having to go into work, but as I looked around my apartment, I had a realization. My life had turned into a real-life *Grey Gardens*. I had been living in filth for the last three-odd days. There were chicken bones and pizza boxes all over the place. The trash hadn't been taken out for days and there was crap everywhere. I looked around and realized that this was it. This was what I had imagined my adulthood to be all along. I was thrilled to be living in filth, and continued to lay around with Sally for the remainder of the day.

Happiness, however, never lasts forever. The two of us could only live in filth for so long before it was time to grow up. After living together for two years, Sally and I left La Boulaie. I was sad to go, but the place was honestly a shit hole and it was time to move on. I'm sure every deliveryman on the Upper East Side misses us, and the fact that we put them all in a new tax bracket, even if only for a few months.

ALL SHOOK UP

There's something about other people's bodily fluids that haunts our heroine. For one reason or another, people with either incontinence or acid reflux problems seem to find Mark in mysterious ways. On one particular summer day in 2005, Mark was pushed too far when a demon child found her way into Mark's life and changed it forever.

All throughout college, I had the good fortune of handing out flyers at the half-price theater ticket booth in the middle of Times Square. It was my job to persuade unsuspecting tourists into seeing the shows that I promoted. It was pretty easy. For one reason or another the idiots who strolled into Times Square looking for theater tickets always listened to whatever I said and I was good at what I did. I took pride in the fact that I could convince moronic hillbillies from Alabama that *Good Vibrations,* the Beach Boys musical, was going to change their lives forever.

During the summer of 2005 I was also working for a little Broadway show called *All Shook Up*. The show took twenty-five of Elvis Presley's biggest hits and threw them into a Shakespeare-themed musical. I loved Elvis and I loved Shakespeare, so as far as I was concerned, this was quite possibly the greatest musical I had ever seen. I loved this show and told anyone who would listen to go and see it.

One particularly hot summer day, a burly couple and their daughter who were looking for theater tickets approached me at the ticket booth. At first glance, I thought they were a lesbian couple, but as they got closer, I realized they were just poorly dressed.

"Hello," the man said. "We're looking for tickets to *The Phantom of the Opera*."

"Why?" I asked.

"Because we want to see it," he replied.

"No, you don't," I said.

"Yes, we do."

"No. You want to go and see *All Shook Up,* the Elvis musical. Trust me. You won't regret it."

"What's it about?" the woman asked.

"Who cares? It's Elvis. When a musical featuring the songs of Elvis is on Broadway, you go and see it."

"Whatever," the man said. "How do we get tickets?"

"You have to get in line," I said as I gestured to the massive line of people waiting for tickets behind me. "It won't take you more than forty-five minutes."

The man, his wife, and their daughter got in line. I noticed that their daughter looked particularly queasy. It was a super hot day out, one for the record books. When I decide I care about my fellow man, which is sporadic at best, I like to check out a certain situation to make sure everything is legit and everyone involved is operating properly. I wondered what was wrong with this poorly dressed couple's child that made her look that way. I made my way through the tourists to find my new hillbilly friends.

"HEY," I yelled.

"We know, we know. *All Shook Up* is going to be a life-changing experience—we got it."

"I'm not worried about that. I know you're going to love the show. Everybody does," I said. "I am concerned about your daughter."

"Why?" the man said.

"She looks like she may be getting sick," I replied. "It's really hot out. Do you want me to grab her a bottle of water or something?"

"She'll be fine," the woman said. "We just got in today and she had a big lunch. She's probably just tired and needs to nap. We'll go back to the hotel after we get our tickets, but thanks for your concern."

I looked at the little girl deep in her eyes. He appearance was reminiscent of what that little bitch from *The Bad Seed* looked like. Besides that, this young lady, who couldn't have been more than ten years old, looked like she was turning a shade of yellow. It almost looked like she had a severe case of jaundice. Having just gone through this with Jessica on *One Life to Live* earlier in the year, I knew a bottle of water and a nap were exactly what this girl needed.

I ran across the street to the deli, leaving my coworkers to fend for themselves, and grabbed a bottle of water for my new friend. It happens about quarterly, and when something horrible happens at the half-price ticket booth I feel as though it's my duty to correct the wrongs of Times Square. I also saw a lot of myself in this little girl. She was overweight, poorly dressed, and had two spastic parents. If she had an affinity for Susan Lucci, I would have thought she was my intellectual equal. I brought the bottle of water back to the little girl.

"Thank you, but that was not necessary," the woman said.

"Well, she looks a little yellow in the face," I replied.

The little girl took the bottle of water and chugged it down as if she was fighting off some sort of bad hangover. Her parents watched in awe.

"Cindy, are you all right?" the woman asked.

"I'm okay, Mom," Cindy said.

I watched as Cindy then began to shake uncontrollably. Normally, I would have lost interest in what was going on and left to smoke a few cigarettes and get a Pop-Tart, but I felt connected to Cindy. Suddenly, her face went from yellow to green.

"I think you guys should skip the show and get little Cindy here out of the heat. What do you say?" I said.

"She's going to be fine. Don't worry about it. We can take it from here," the woman said. I began to walk away in hopes that my beloved Cindy wouldn't meet her maker in line to get theater tickets. I mean I loved *All Shook Up* as much as the next guy, but I wasn't willing to die to get tickets. Or was I?

"Wait!" Cindy said as she grabbed the back of my shirt.

I turned around and bent down to meet Cindy at her level. She was such a little cutie. As I looked at her, I could see her face was turning from green back to a healthy yellow.

"Thank you," Cindy said.

"Awww . . . you're welcome, honey," I replied.

"Thank you for the . . ." She paused.

Suddenly, I could see something well up inside of her. As

Cindy tried to finish her sentence, she literally could not talk. It was as if the devil was inside of her. Perhaps she was the little girl from *The Bad Seed* live and in person.

"Thank you for the..." She paused again. Her parents looked at her. Being on Cindy's level, I looked up at her parents. When I tilted my head back to meet Cindy's eyes, she opened her mouth and projectile-vomited all over my face.

"OH MY GOD!" I yelled.

Her mother looked horrified, but I think her father may have been chuckling.

"WHAT THE FUCK?" I screamed. "What the fuck is wrong with your daughter?"

"I think she may have eaten too much at the Olive Garden," her mother said. Why tourists continue to eat at the Olive Garden when there are so many amazing Italian restaurants in New York is still beyond me.

"I'm feeling much better, Mommy," Cindy said.

I gave them the finger and hailed the first cab I could find.

"Thirty-fourth and Eighth, please. As fast as you can get there!" I yelled.

The Persian cab driver turned around and looked at me.

"What the hell happened to you?" he asked.

"A child just threw up all over my face! Can you please focus on the road and take me home. NOW!" I yelled.

"Oh, no, that's horrible," the cab driver said. "The smell of throw-up makes me want to throw up."

"OH GOD!" I yelled. "Please don't." Suddenly, I remembered that the smell of throw-up made me want to throw up as well. I sat in the back of the cab, covered in a little girl's vomit, trying not to vomit myself. Because I was being personally tested that day, my possibly retarded cab driver took Ninth Avenue, which was bumper to bumper.

"Is there any way we could move this along?"

"I'm sorry," he said. "I'm trying to get you out of my cab as quickly as I can."

I concluded that it would be best if I got rid of everything I was wearing to try and get rid of the smell. I took my shirt off and threw it out the window.

"WHAT ARE YOU DOING?" the cab driver yelled.

"TAKING MY CLOTHES OFF!" I yelled.

"You're going to get me fined," he said.

"Well, it's either that, or we both throw up all over the place."

The people in the cars next to me were looking in my cab as if I was putting on some sort of peep show. If only they knew what was actually going on. Damn Cindy and her Olive Garden–eating parents. I vowed revenge.

After getting rid of my clothes, the cab still smelled like throw-up. I could tell my cab driver was now feeling the smell and was beginning to get nauseous himself. Come to think of it, I was feeling pretty sick as well. Our cab was still only on Fortieth Street. I was now not only covered in vomit but shirt-less as well. It was too many blocks to walk. Meanwhile, the cab driver decided to roll down all of the windows in the cab to air out the smell, which, when you're in a cab that's going nowhere in 103-degree heat, only makes it worse.

I was disgusted with myself. I double-checked my driver to make sure he was okay.

"How's it going up there, buddy?"

"Don't buddy me," he said. "You smell like shit. You owe

me fifty dollars. I am going to have to get my cab cleaned extra special now."

What I should have told him to do was fuck off. Instead, I gave him fifty dollars and told him to book it to my place as fast as he could.

As we inched closer to my apartment, I thought I'd make it back to my place relatively unscathed. When we turned the cab onto Thirty-fourth Street, I felt relieved. I had almost made it home and neither the cab driver nor I got sick. As I reached into my other pocket to get my keys out, I stuck my hand into a pocket that was filled with vomit. Somehow, Cindy's vomit had made its way into my pocket as well. That was enough to throw me off the edge.

"I gotta get out! Now!"

"I can't pull over here," he replied. I felt vomit welling up inside me. Before I could stick my head out of the window, I vomited all over the guarder between the cab driver and me. Had that plastic window not been up, the driver would have been covered in puke as well.

"Goddamn it! Goddamn it! Goddamn it!"

I jumped out of the car and began running, shirtless, back to my apartment building. I had already given the cab driver fifty bucks to clean his cab and felt that a thirty-five-dollar tip sufficed the fact that I had thrown up all over his car.

"Mark," said the doorman as he gave me the once-over. "Are you hammered right now?"

"It's three o'clock in the afternoon," I replied.

"It's Saturday," he said.

"Oh, I didn't think of that. I would tell you what just happened to me but you wouldn't believe it."

I went up to my apartment and showered for two and a half hours.

The next day, Cindy and her hillbilly parents swung by the half-price tickets booth to apologize. I did not accept the apology and told them that their daughter's digestive tract had sparked a chain of events that cost me not only fifty dollars but a Diesel shirt, neither of which they were interested in reimbursing me for. Had I not once been that little girl who ate too much at the Olive Garden on a hot summer day, I would have been pissed.

THE FLYER BOY FOLLIES

After college was over, our beloved heroine found himself in quite the quandary. How was he supposed to support himself while trying to fulfill his lifelong dream of becoming a famous author? After waiting tables, telemarketing, and a brief foray in prostitution didn't work, Mark found himself standing back in the middle of Times Square handing out flyers while being tempted by the evil seductions of every chain restaurant that ever existed. Will our champion Mark be able to survive his job and keep his dignity?

When I published my first book, I was saddened to find out that I was still going to have work full time. Apparently, the Jackie Collins style of living I had hoped for was going to have to wait. Luckily I have a job handing out flyers outside of the half-price ticket booth in Times Square. The money is good, but since jobs are scarce, people get stuck working there for a long time. Meanwhile, Broadway is dying for the fourteenth time this year, and the only shows that any tourist wants to see are the wildly popular ones with big advertising budgets (*Wicked, Jersey Boys,* etc.). More than half of the tourists who come to the half-price ticket booth are looking for discounted tickets for sold-out shows, so it becomes my job to try and coax them into seeing one of the shows that I work for. This is a clear example of how capitalism continues to screw me. The following is a typical day at the half-price ticket booth. Welcome to hell.

Wednesday, December 2

8 a.m.: I wake up, brush my teeth, and take a shower. It's Wednesday, so it's a matinee day. Meaning there are two shows today and an eleven-hour day ahead of me.

8:20 a.m.: I get dressed. First I put on two pairs of underwear; it's going to be a cold day so I need to make sure my Johnson doesn't freeze. Then I put on a pair of long johns, a pair of sweatpants, and a pair of jeans over that. Then I put on a T-shirt, two thermals, two hoodies, and a coat. Finally, I put on four pairs of socks. I put plastic bags over the socks before I put them into my shoes. It's going to rain today so I need to make sure my feet don't get wet; it's a little trick I learned from a homeless man named Felix. Anyone watching as I attempt to put my shoes on over four pairs of socks and plastic bags would have had a stroke from laughing. I fall over twice, then realize that I look homeless as I glance in the mirror. No time to think of that now, I need to get to work.

. . .

8:45 a.m.: After grabbing the biggest cup of coffee I can find, I put my earphones in and blast Britney Spears on my iPod. I need to get pumped for the day that lies ahead, and no one can do that better than Brit.

9:30 a.m.: I arrive at work. The half-price ticket booth is located in the middle of Times Square, on Forty-seventh Street between Broadway and Seventh Avenue, and is surrounded on all sides by cars. Meaning I literally spend my day playing in traffic while handing out flyers. Not only am I handing out flyers in the middle of the largest intersection on the East Coast, every fifteen seconds there is a toothless homeless person screaming for money or fourteen fire trucks zooming by blasting their sirens requiring me to scream over all of the noise to be heard. I thought there was a law against adding to the noise pollution in New York, but apparently I was wrong. By the time I've arrived, I am sweating my ass off from sitting on a subway car while wearing fourteen layers of clothes.

9:31 a.m.: "Do you have tickets to *Wicked*?" I'm asked the first question of the day and am already annoyed. "I am sorry, ma'am, we do not sell *Wicked* tickets here, you have to go to the theater," I reply. "Oh, you mean I have to pay full price?" What a concept.

9:44 a.m.: I begin handing out flyers to the people in line. Today I am telling everyone to go see *The 39 Steps,* a rollicking comedy based on the Alfred Hitchcock film. I start working the line and a woman stops me. "Excuse me, sir," she says. "Can you take this for me?" she asks as she hands me her garbage. "I am sorry, miss, but I am not a trash can," I reply. "Well I don't want it," she says as she throws her garbage at me. Seriously? We're going to play this game right now? I pick up the garbage that she just threw at me and throw it in her face. "Fuck you," I reply. "Oh, and go see *The 39 Steps*," I say as I throw a flyer her way.

9:47 a.m.: I tell all of the other flyer people about the bitch who is coming their way. I have to repeat myself twelve times because a brigade of police cars roars past us causing a minor scene with the tourists who automatically think another terrorist attack is going down.

9:59 a.m.: The little old ladies have come out in droves. They love matinees. It's a chance for them to see the revival of *Bye, Bye Birdie* before they die . . . later that day. It's not uncommon to hear things such as, "Gladys, remember when we saw the original *South Pacific* on Broadway? What a show!" or "Teddy Roosevelt—now *that* was a president." And the best part about matinees is that all of the old women love me. I always remind them of a great-great grandson, so they naturally listen when I tell them to see the new revival of *Finian's Rainbow*.

10:14 a.m.: I begin contemplating what I am going to have for lunch. There are so many possibilities. I am literally surrounded by options. McDonald's, T.G.I. Fridays, Olive Garden, Dunkin' Donuts, Applebee's, and Famous Dave's. It's like being stuck in the worst shopping mall in America.

10:45 a.m.: I am smoking my seventeenth cigarette of the day when asked, "Do you have tickets for *Jersey Boys?*" I say no and promptly blow smoke in the unknowing tourist's face. The only perk of this job is that I can smoke cigarettes freely. That is until Bloomberg bans smoking outside too.

10:46 a.m.: "Do you have tickets for *Jersey Boys?*" "No."

10:47 a.m.: "Do you have tickets for *Jersey Boys?*" "No."

10:47 1/2 a.m.: "Do you have tickets for *Jersey Boys?*" "Go fuck yourself." It's all about the customer service.

11:13 a.m.: The one inch of my body that is not covered up begins to freeze and I assume that if it is not covered immediately, I will die of pneumonia within minutes. I dart across the street to Forever 21 (I never imagined I would ever say "Thank God for Forever 21" more than once in my life, but here we are) to grab an extra scarf. On my way back to the booth, I grab a hot dog from a street vendor (I know I'm taking a gamble with my health in doing so, but it's going to be a long day and food poisoning is always an amazing excuse to leave work) and almost get hit by a McDonald's truck crossing the street. That would have been an ironic way to go down, but no such luck today.

11:34 a.m.: A lovely Spanish couple comes to the booth but they don't speak any English. I tell them to go see my favorite show, *Burn the Floor*, because it's all dancing and singing and no speaking. I begin a pantomime demonstration of what the show is by attempting to flail my arms as if I'm dancing, but I am wearing so many goddamn layers it looks like I'm just bobbing my head around like a creepy jack-in-the-box. After a minute, when they still don't understand what I am doing, I just start yelling *"¡EL FUEGO! ¡EL FUEGO!"* and send them on their way.

12:31 p.m.: The matinee is flying by. I just sent a lovely Japanese couple that didn't speak a lick of English to see David Mamet's new play, *Race*. They aren't going to understand what the fuck is going on, but apparently James Spader is huge in Japan and when they saw he was in it, they flipped out. I pat myself on the back for a job well done.

12:46 p.m.: I saw him. My new husband. Tall, dark, handsome, and probably doesn't speak any English. I inadvertently blow smoke in his face and ask if he has any questions about any of the shows. He glances at me and smiles. He is probably smiling because he notices that due to my many layers, I can barely lift my arms. It must be love.

. . .

1:24 p.m.: The boss calls. We have a twelve-minute conversation about what happened on *One Life to Live* the day before. I yell, "EXCUSE ME?" "I'M SORRY, WHAT DID YOU SAY?" and "WHAT?" into the phone repeatedly because a homeless man who refuses to take no for an answer continues to bother me for a quarter while I'm on the phone. The boss tells me to come to the theater when I am on break so we can chain-smoke.

1:36 p.m.: I saw him. My *new* new husband. All thoughts of the hot foreigner are erased as a hottie with blond hair asks me where *Mamma Mia!* is. Terrible taste in theater, but gorgeous nonetheless. I follow him with my eyes as he goes to the window to buy his tickets. He kisses his girlfriend after the purchase.

1:55 p.m.: "Do you have tickets for *Jersey Boys?*" "Sorry, I am on my lunch break."

2:01–2:29 p.m.: I go to Famous Dave's, just across the street, and literally go downtown on a chicken sandwich.

2:34 p.m.: After some quick gossip with the girls from the typing pool, it's back to work. Someone asks me where *Jersey Boys* is playing and I almost lose it. It's too early into the evening shift to go completely ballistic so I point them in the right direction. When I am at the half-price ticket booth, it's almost as if I am an air traffic controller. I point in the direction the theaters are because most of the people I am talking to don't speak any fucking English. Yesterday I was pointing two little Japanese girls—who I swear were Hollaback girls in one of Gwen Stefani's music videos—to the *Phantom of the Opera* theater when I literally backhanded a man in the face. He crept right up on me. It felt good, but the Japanese girls still had no idea where the fuck they were going.

2:59 p.m.: Boss texts me to make sure I call him after I watch *One Life to Live* when I get home that night.

3:09 p.m.: I begin flyering the line with *Next to Normal* flyers. A woman stops to ask me a question. "So, are you guys, like, in the shows?" she asks. "Yes. That's me," I say as I point to the lead guy's face on the *Next to Normal* flyer. "I have nothing better to do but come out here on my free time between shows and moonlighting on *Gossip Girl*. Come see me!" I say as I hand her a flyer. Idiot.

4:14 p.m.: "Do you have tickets for *Jersey Boys*?" So we're doing this again, are we?

4:34 p.m.: "Who pays you?" a fat-ass Alabama native asks. Since I am simply standing on a street corner, holding court in plain clothes, many tourists wonder why the fuck they should listen to me anyway. As if it makes one bit of fucking difference, I reply, "Some of the shows." I always want to answer: "If you knew what the fuck you were doing, you wouldn't need to ask for advice, so what fucking difference does it make who pays me?" but I refrain from doing so.

5:05 p.m.: Apparently the woman I threw the *39 Steps* flyer at went to see the show and loved it. I may have to add that technique to the repertoire.

5:14 p.m.: I saw him. My *new*, new husband. Absolutely gorgeous. He asks me if we have tickets for *Jersey Boys*. He was so hot that I didn't even care he was asking a dumb question.

5:46 p.m.: A woman walks up to me and asks me where the theater for *Billy Elliot* is. After she finishes her sentence, she begins sniffing around and gives me a look that says: "Did you just rip one while I was asking you a question?" Knowing she was probably too polite to ask such a question, I reply to her face by saying: "I didn't fart if you were wondering. This lovely ticket booth was built right on top of the sewer. Those are the sweet smells of New York, my dear, I can't take credit for that."

6 p.m.: My arm starts to tingle. I come up with a list of things that could possibly be wrong with me: 1. The seventy-eighth cigarette that I just smoked today is going to be the one that gives me a heart attack. 2. My circulation is cut off from all of the layers of clothes that I am wearing. 3. I am about to stroke out from looking at the American Eagle billboard that is ten stories tall and constantly flashes random colors and lights onto Times Square. I pick option three and stop looking above me.

6:16 p.m.: A crazy man comes up and tells me that the rapture is coming on May 22, 2011. I find this interesting because when we last spoke the rapture was not coming until sometime in December 2012. I make a note of it and move on with my day.

6:28 p.m.: I am cold and wet and people keep asking me about the twenty-dollar tickets to *The Lion King* that don't exist. I think of possible scenarios that could have happened in another life that led me to the indentured servitude that is my present state. I must have killed a baby or invaded Poland or something terrible to lead me here. I ask the tourists looking for shows if they know of anyone who is hiring.

6:46 p.m.: I tell a group of teenagers that *The Marvelous Wonderettes,* the fifties pop musical, will change their lives forever. They buy ten tickets.

6:49 p.m.: "Wrecked?" a tourist asks. "What?" I reply. "Uhhhh...Wrecked?" he asks again. "What?" "Ummm .... wrecked?" he says again as he points to the billboard for *Wicked*. "Oh, *Wicked*!" I reply. "Nope, no tickets here." If you can't pronounce the show you want to see then you have no business going to see it as far as I am concerned, but I told him where the theater was anyway. I also told him where *Jersey Boys* tickets were, to prevent him coming back to ask any more questions.

6:51 p.m.: Some redneck asks me if the *Wicked* theater is behind Tad's Steaks. I tell her that the sign she's looking at is just an advertisement on top of the restaurant, not a two-thousand-seat theater.

7:04 p.m.: The woman who has only one tooth who scalps tickets asks me if I want to buy an illegal ticket to *Ragtime*. I tell her I work here, as I have on and off for the better part of a decade, and she suddenly remembers and flees. We do this daily.

7:09 p.m.: I meet my newest husband. He doesn't know I love him, but I soon realize that no one will fall in love with me if I continue to dress like the kid from *A Christmas Story*. After he departs, a smell wafts from the Olive Garden across the street. It smells a bit of fettuccini Alfredo and I begin to weigh my dinner options.

7:30 p.m.: The final countdown begins. It's a half hour to show time and I tell people to hustle up and hit the showers, as if we were all about to, or had just played a football game. As I am doing this, a man approaches and I ask if he has any questions. He tells me that he is a New Yorker and doesn't need my help. I give him a dirty look and his tune quickly changes. "Excuse me," he says. "Do you have tickets for *Cats*?" I begin laughing uproariously. Toward the end of an eleven-hour day, after seven cups of coffee, the smallest things can turn into a laugh riot. "I thought you said you were a New Yorker," I say gasping for air. I'm literally hysterical as I continue: "That show has been closed for ten years you stupid piece of shit!" I continue laughing. "But you're a New Yorker, you know *everything*, don't you?" I laugh until I almost fall over and the man walks away in shame.

7:39 p.m.: I am bored so I contemplate getting my eighth cup of coffee of the day.

7:40 p.m.: "Do you sell tickets for *Jersey Boys*?" "Go to hell!"

7:59 p.m.: It's quitting time. I get on the subway to go home.

8:23 p.m.: I get off the subway and have swamp ass again. Going from hot to cold and back again is going to give me pneumonia by New Year's.

8:49 p.m.: I am on the couch with a bucket of chicken watching *One Life to Live,* dreading doing all of this over again tomorrow. So maybe things aren't all that bad. I have a job—it's an annoying one, but it's a job nonetheless. At least I can still afford fancy dinners, and my soap operas will always be free.

TUESDAYS WITH RICKY

Keeping up with the Joneses is exhausting. As Mark continued to try his best to look good, he began to realize that he could no longer do it on his own. He needed someone to guide him along his path in finding the perfect body. Not only did it turn out to be someone our heroine wanted to sleep with, but he reminded him of someone who had always complained about his weight in the past. If Freud were still alive, he'd most likely have his hands full with this one.

When I stopped drinking, I made it a point to hit the gym as much as possible. I've said it before and I'll say it again, no one likes a fattie, especially one who spends his afternoons in a room full of alcoholics trying to stay sober. In an effort to not revert back to my old ways of being a complete fat-ass (I was supplementing booze with food for a bit and the results were seam splitting), I joined the Midtown Health and

Racquet in Times Square. Every afternoon I would hit the gym and was constantly surrounded by every chorus boy Broadway had to offer. Each body was more ripped than the next, and I was quickly becoming more self-conscious than ever. After a few weeks I decided it was time to put a personal trainer on the payroll in order to fast-track the results I desired.

One Tuesday, I began to weigh my options in the personal-trainer department. There was the pretty blond girl named Lindsay who was always training the blind guy who was there every time I was at the gym. Being gay and going to the gym was obnoxious enough, but not being able to see must have made it an absolute nightmare. He wasn't able to actually see the hot guys at the gym judging him, which must have made his hour at the gym devastating. Then there was Corey, the deaf trainer. He seemed very friendly and very fit, but it always seemed as though he had trouble communicating with his clients. Then there was Ricky. Ricky was about my height, five eight, tan with a short military haircut and built like a brick shit house. There was something about Ricky that drew me to him. I wanted to sleep with him.

"Excuse me," I said as I tapped Ricky on the shoulder as he was about to enter his office.

"What's up?" he said.

My heart was aflutter. He was gorgeous.

"Ummm..." I said. "I wanted to inquire about using your services."

Suddenly I felt like every Japanese businessmen who ever ordered a hooker from an escort agency.

"All right yo," he said as he gestured me toward his office. "Take a seat."

Ricky sat down on the adjacent chair and I stared at him. He was the most handsome man I had ever seen.

"I'm Ricky," he said as he stuck his hand out to meet mine. I grabbed his hand, shook it, and then put it to my nose to smell his sweet manly scent. He quickly pulled his hand out of mine. "What can I help you with?"

"Well, I want to get back into shape," I said.

Ricky gave me the once-over and replied: "It looks like you're in pretty good shape to me."

I blushed and tried to gather my bearings. His awesomeness was entirely too overwhelming. I was going to need a cold shower and a Kit Kat in order to calm down. Since neither were readily available, I replied, "Thanks." I was blushing to the point that it must have looked like my head was going to explode.

"So what the fuck do you want with me?" Ricky said.

I wanna fuck you! I thought, but kept my big mouth shut.

"Uh." I didn't know what to say. Suddenly, my badass attitude came thundering back. If I was going to train with Ricky, I was going to have to get my shit together and pronto.

"Listen, Ricky," I said. "I know I am in okay shape, but I want to be in the best shape possible. I need to find a man, and fast, and the only way to do that in this town is with a good body. I'm roaring into my late twenties and I'm basically in a race to make sure that I don't die alone. And considering the fact that I have spent the last decade of my life chasing after every unavailable man in the tri-state area to the point that I could teach a class at the goddamned Learning Annex on how to date losers, I need to make sure that my body is in check so that I can start attracting a better class of men."

Ricky laughed uproariously. "You are one funny son of a bitch!"

I told him that if he thought that was funny, then he would

certainly need to read my book, so following my outburst we ordered it on his computer.

"Anyway," Ricky then said, "tell me about your diet."

"Well..." I trailed off. I couldn't possibly tell my new best friend that I had just eaten half a cake for breakfast, so I did what I did best: I lied to his face. "You know, for breakfast I eat eggs usually [lie], for lunch I usually eat a sensible salad [lie—unless you consider the lettuce and tomato on top of a hamburger a salad], and for dinner I usually eat chicken or fish [not a complete lie unless someone had pissed me off that day, in which case I would eat a whole pizza myself]."

"Sounds pretty good," Ricky said. I was starting this relationship off on a lie, as I had with every other relationship I had been in up to now. Perhaps it wasn't my body that was keeping me from having a boyfriend. Perhaps it was my big flapping mouth.

I smiled at Ricky. He smiled back.

"Do you mind if I order lunch while we have this conversation?" Ricky asked.

"No, of course not."

Ricky dialed the phone and put it to his ear. Before anyone picked up on the other end he whispered to me: "Fucking Chinese people. At least they're good for something."

Once the Chinese restaurant picked up on the other end, Ricky then ordered everything off the menu. He was a man after my own heart, a borderline racist with an insatiable hunger for the food made by people he claimed to hate.

After ordering what seemed like seven hundred dollars' worth of food, Ricky turned to me and asked if I wanted anything.

"A few dumplings never killed anyone, now have they?" I asked.

"They sure as shit haven't."

"Great," I replied. "I'll have twelve."

As I sat and watched Ricky give the restaurant his credit card information, all I could think was that Ricky eerily reminded me of someone, but I couldn't put my finger on whom. Ricky loved Chinese food, had a touch of racism, and was sure to be calling me fat and making me hustle around the gymnasium for hours on end. I soon realized that I was about to pay someone hundreds of dollars to do what someone had done for me for free for twenty-seven years: make me feel fat and inadequate. I was paying Ricky to replace my father, and apparently my stepmother as well.

"I'm fucking starving, man!" Ricky said as he hung up the phone.

"Do you always eat this much?" I asked.

"Yeah, pretty much," he replied, "but I work out like a motherfucker."

"You curse even more than I do," I said as I gazed into his eyes.

"Yeah, I was in the military for like four fucking years. All they do there is curse. And shoot things. I miss it."

"Right," I said. "So you think you can help me?"

"Of course."

Ricky explained that he thought it would be best if we did a series of drills he had learned in the military. They were excruciating, but he promised that if I kept it up, the results would be amazing.

When the food arrived and I got a waft of an eggroll, I

was suddenly transported back to elementary school. I've always associated Chinese food with my father. Many years ago at our favorite Chinese restaurant he'd revealed that he had gotten married in a secret ceremony without any of his children present. Since then, my relationship with Chinese food had not been the same.

After stuffing our faces and talking about who we wanted to have sex with at the gym (which was pretty much everyone for me), Ricky and I agreed to meet every Tuesday.

I will never forget my first session with Ricky. I met him in the dance studio at the gym. There were three punching bags in the middle of the floor. On the sides of the room were weights and staking steps. I had no idea what I was in for, but I was already regretting the three cupcakes I had eaten for breakfast.

"Hey, fucker!" Ricky said as I entered the dance studio.

"What the hell is going on in here?"

Ricky explained that I would be dragging all three punching bags from one end of the room to the other. Once there, I would lift the weights that were set aside for me, then I would hit the floor and do crunches while placing the staking steps from one side of me to the other. After I was finished with that, I was to drag the punching bags back to the end of the room, do forty jumping jacks, forty squats, and forty push-ups.

Once he finished going over our routine, I laughed, because I thought he was kidding. He wasn't.

"Seems like a lot of work to me," I said.

"You want a boyfriend, right?"

I nodded.

"Then get your ass to work."

"Can we listen to music at least?" I asked.

"Sure."

"Britney Spears?"

"Fuck no."

"Gangster rap?"

"Duh!"

"Good. I can only listen to Britney or O.D.B. while I'm working out."

After plugging my iPod into the stereo system and blasting "Shimmy Shimmy Ya" as loud as I possibly could, I began dragging the first punching bag from one end of the room to the other. Before I had even made it halfway, I paused.

"Why are you stopping?" Ricky asked.

"Out." I paused. "I'm out of . . ."

"WHAT?"

"I'M OUT OF BREATH!" I yelled.

"Do you smoke?"

"Yes."

"You need to quit. Gay boys these days don't like smokers."

"How the fuck do you even know that?" I said as I continued to drag the punching bag across the floor. But it was true: The gays are so health-conscious these days. Apparently, they think it's more socially acceptable to smoke crystal meth than cigarettes.

"I have a lot of gay clients," Ricky said. "In fact, one of them took me out to a gay bar. Did you know that Britney Spears sang a song about getting naked? I found it very distasteful."

"Are you kidding me right now?" I asked. This was coming from a man who moments earlier had explained in great detail what he wanted to do sexually to one of the female personal trainers, but continued that if he had done these things she would get "too attached because that's what stupid women tend to do." "Let's not talk about distasteful right now," I said.

I continued huffing and puffing and Ricky continued chiming in with his ridiculous segues.

"You know what doesn't suck though?" Ricky asked.

"I don't remember asking, but what?"

"Smoking weed. I smoked the biggest blunt last night. I got so high that I literally ate everything in my refrigerator and the only things in there were a pack of batteries and a jar of mayonnaise."

After having carried one punching bag across the floor, I stopped dead in my tracks, already dripping with sweat, and looked Ricky dead in the eyes.

"YOU ARE THE DUMBEST PIECE OF SHIT I'VE EVER MET," I yelled.

Suddenly, his face went from being completely lax to that of a creepy jack-in-the-box and he began laughing hysterically.

"I know, man, I was so high." He couldn't control his laughter.

"Are you high right now?" I asked.

Suddenly he stopped laughing and got very serious. "A little, but don't tell anyone."

After an hour of dragging things, jumping jacks, and thinking that Ricky was actually out to kill me rather than help me, our session was over. I had asked Ricky if a shower with the personal trainer was included in the package and he told me to fuck off.

The following Tuesday, I was greeted at the gym by Ricky, who was eating the biggest bowl of pasta I had ever seen.

"Seriously?" I asked.

"Yeah," he replied, with pasta sauce on the side of his cheek. "I like to eat shit in front of people at the gym to make them feel bad about themselves."

Ricky was such an asshole and quite possibly the greatest person I had met in my life. I soon realized that the two of us together would be unstoppable and invited him to a party I was throwing later that week.

"Are there going to be hot girls there?" he asked.

"Duh," I replied. "I'm gay. I only hang out with hot girls. Just keep your mouth shut or none of them will want anything to do with you."

After shooting the shit for a bit, Ricky explained what to-day's workout was going to entail. I was going to be lugging shit up fifteen flights of steps and back, while he supervised.

"This sounds awful."

"Just fucking do what I tell you!" he replied. As I began my journey, Ricky began ranting. The man had a way with words that was unbounded. That day I got to learn a little bit more about the man I had so quickly come to admire.

Ricky on personal hygiene:

"You know what's good about people who stink at the gym?" he asked.

"What?"

"Fucking nothing, man. They need to take a shower. When I was in the military we shared our gym with a bunch of fucking Germans and it's like they never showered. They stunk like shit, man. I hate Germans."

Ricky on dating:

"So last weekend I got shit-faced at this restaurant with this Albanian girl. She was hot, but I got the feeling she wasn't going to put out so I ended up getting head from the hostess at the restaurant we were at."

Ricky on Washington Heights:

"I just don't get why Dominican people feel the need to always sit on my stoop. Get your own goddamn stoop. Also, have you ever wondered why people who don't speak English feel the need to talk so much goddamn louder than everyone else? What the fuck?"

He just kept talking as I kept running up and down flights of stairs. The man would not shut up.

As I made my final lap up the stairs, I yelled, "DO YOU EVER SHUT THE FUCK UP?"

Again, Ricky began to laugh as if the devil was inside of him.

"No, man, I don't."

"Are you high right now?" I asked.

"A little," he replied.

I crawled to the shower after our workout. Looking good for the ladies was more difficult than I had expected it was going to be.

Our final Tuesday together (because I was too cheap to pay

for more than three workouts) was pretty simple. Ricky took me around the gym and we lifted weights "the right way," as he liked to say. After our workout, Ricky took me into his office. Hoping for another tour of China, I sat down in anticipation of a feeding frenzy.

"So," Ricky said. "I started training this guy Mike. Mike Sinatra."

"Is he related to Frank Sinatra?" I asked.

"That's what I asked," he replied. "And he was like, 'No, I am not related to Frank Sinatra.' I told him that the next time someone asked him if he was related to Frank Sinatra to tell them to go fuck themselves because it's none of their goddamn business."

"Uh, okay," I said.

"Anyway, he's gay and I thought you two could hook up."

"Are you setting me up on a blind date?" I asked. "What makes you think I will like him?"

"I don't know," he replied. "You're both gay." After not having been touched by a man in what felt like a decade, that was a good enough reason for me.

"Anyway, I told him all about you and he's interested in meeting you."

"Seriously?" I asked, "You're orchestrating a gay blind date?"

"Yeah, why the fuck not?"

Ricky is like the straightest person I've ever known, and since I am the gayest person I know, I found our relationship very interesting. He was in serious contention for new best friendship.

"All right, well, set it up," I said.

"Fine, but only if you find me some pussy."

"Fuck off," I said as I closed the door to his office after walking out.

Next week at the gym, I met Mike Sinatra and quickly learned that he had nothing to say for himself. I tried to get him to talk, but he was having none of it. Just because two people are gay does not a match make. Ricky, if you're reading this, I hope you've learned a valuable lesson.

After spending hundreds of dollars on a personal trainer, I soon realized that if I want to be spoken to like shit and told that I am fat, I can just call one of my various family members on the phone and have them do that for me for free.

THE JOY OF SEX

After finishing his first book and being rejected by nearly every agent in New York City, our heroine was left with an ax to grind and the urge to begin thinking outside the box. Mark had a wonderful book that needed to be published, but he couldn't figure out how until he channeled Julia Child and came up with a delicious idea.

When I was trying to get my first book published, I took some pretty drastic measures. One summer evening, I decided to take a break and catch a movie. The movie I picked was *Julie and Julia* starring Amy Adams of *Drop Dead Gorgeous* fame. According to the film, some homely chick named Julie Powell decided that she was going to prepare every recipe in Julia Child's masterpiece, *Mastering the Art of French Cooking,* and blog about it every day. Powell ended up turning her blog into a bestselling novel and subsequently into a film that made a shit-ton of money. The only thing I got out of this movie was that the best way to get people to notice you is to steal someone else's idea. Since I am not above stealing other people's ideas, I decided that I was going to do precisely what Julie Powell did and put a new spin on an old favorite. All I needed to do was find a respected and well-known book that was familiar and that most Americans knew. After weeks of racking my brain and trying to think of whom to plagiarize, I realized that it was there all along. I could read Alex Comfort's *The Joy of Sex* and blog about every sexual position in the book.

After patting myself on the back for coming up with such an amazing epiphany, I realized that in order for me to blog about all of the sexual positions in *The Joy of Sex,* I would actually need a partner for this. I had cleaned up my alcoholic ways and got sober, and pretty much stopped having sex altogether. Granted, I had never looked better, but I had begun to hate people, in general, more than ever. I decided that the best thing to do would be to go online and see if anyone would be game. Since all gay men are pretty much whores, I thought this task would be effortless. I went to Manhunt, an online site where gay guys meet to get it on. Our generation has completely cut out all forms of personal contact in meeting, so I thought in order to find someone to go along with my latest scheme, Manhunt would be the way to go. However, I am too paranoid to actually seek out guys and usually get sidetracked, so I wait for people to seek me out. The only problem is that the only people looking for me are either men over forty or creepy-looking guys who look like they randomly drive by high schools with one hand on the steering wheel and another on their stick shift. Finally, after an hour of warding off weirdos, someone normal looking e-mailed me.

His headline read: "Gimme a Kiss." I enjoy kissing strangers, so I continued. "Super chill and fun and polite and smiley. Open to dating but only guys under thirty." He didn't look like a complete tool; in fact he was pretty good looking, so I e-mailed him back. Got to love Manhunt, as conversations usually go something like this:

"Hey," guy one says.

"Hey," guy two says.

"What's up?" guy one says.

"Me," guy two says.

"Wanna come over?" guy one says.

"Sure, where are you located?" guy two says.

It's nothing if not efficient. Anyway, I continued talking to my new friend, whose name was Tom. I found out that he lived in the West Village and was pushing forty. Now I usually do not find myself having much in common with people around forty. Little old Jewish ladies in their late seventies, I could have hour-long conversations with them, but with guys in their forties, I got nothing. I decided to meet Tom to see if he would be an apt candidate for my most recent scheme. He asked to meet me at a café near his apartment to see if we "clicked." I think he wanted to meet in public to make sure I was not a complete psychopath. But I am crazy in public, in private, on a plane, on a train . . . so it really makes no difference where we met, I just had to make sure he didn't catch on to the fact that I was totally using him for my latest project. I certainly could not let Tom know that if he was a fit, we would be getting it on *The Joy of Sex* style, every time we met. This first meeting was just going to be a "test drive."

When we met at the café, he walked up, took one look at me, and said, "Let's go to my place. There are no seats at the café."

"Do you have croissants?" I asked.

He looked dumbfounded. After realizing we had just met and he did not know the heights of my gluttony, I shrugged my shoulders and followed him to his place. I guess he did not find me to be a psychopath because before I knew it I was sitting on his couch and we were chatting. We made the usual small talk, like: What do you do for a living? Where are you from? What do you like to do for fun? All I could do was sit there, wondering why we could not have done this at the café. At least I would have been able to have a little nosh.

Tom rattled on and on about how he loved going to Sandy Hook and all I could do was pray for all of this to be over. It's a shame I love my art as much as I do. This was already taking too long. I had a week's worth of *All My Children* saved on my DVR that was not going to watch itself. I was going out on a total limb in order to get some much-needed buzz for my career and all this guy was doing was yakking about some gay beach in New Jersey. Finally, I walked into his bedroom, plopped down on the bed, and waited for him to come in. I am a decent-looking twenty-six-year-old. Tom was pushing forty and should have been so lucky to have me in his apartment. He quickly followed suit and we did it.

Tom was a pretty okay guy. I had absolutely nothing in common with him, but if I was going to get published, and quickly, I needed to use Tom to get what I wanted. We text-messaged back and forth for a few days. Having already covered chapter 1 in *The Joy of Sex,* "Fellatio," I quickly needed to see Tom again and move on so I could blog about it. But the next weekend, Tom told me he had plans and totally blew me off.

I'm never going to get published. Never! Never! Never! I thought after getting blown off by Tom. But I was always told patience is a virtue, so I decided to wait. I guess I could have just found someone else to have sex with, but that seemed like too much work and I didn't want to get an STD before my first book even came out. Tom texted me that he would be free the following Monday, so I waited for him to make plans.

"Want to hang out?" Tom texted me that Monday.

"Yes!" I replied. I was desperate for material. We had been going back and forth for two weeks and we were still only on chapter 1 of *The Joy of Sex.*

"I just need to let you know something," Tom wrote. "This is only for fun. I am not looking for a relationship."

Ummmm . . . okay. I could not flat-out tell him I was using him for material, because I didn't want to seem like the asshole that I actually am, but I was a little offended that he thought I was interested in him in the first place. He's forty. The only thing I have in common with forty-year-olds is a mutual love of Vicks VapoRub and other various ointments, and perhaps a fondness for eighties prime-time soaps like *Falcon Crest,* but most homos these days don't even appreciate the classics. Who the hell did this guy think he was? Suddenly, my latest project seemed less appetizing than Julia Child's recipe for grilled intestines. I was inadvertently getting my feelings hurt by a guy I was not even interested in. How did this happen?

"Yes, Tom, I understand that this is just for fun," I replied.

"Good," Tom said, "because the last person I wanted to have a casual thing with turned clingy and it ruined everything."

Who did this guy think he was? Annoyed, I said: "I understand, Tom. Just let me know when you're free and we can take it from there."

"Will do," he said.

Thinking our exchange had ended, I turned on the TV and began watching the episodes of *All My Children* that were now backlogged on my DVR. As I glanced up to see Erica Kane in all of her glory, I received yet another text message from Tom.

"I just don't get it!" Tom wrote. "Every time I start talking to a guy, they, like, fall in love with me."

You've got to be kidding me, I thought. Granted, I needed Tom to move on with my project, but he was thoroughly pissing me off.

"Yes, I get it. You're hot. Talk soon," I replied.

"Gosh, I don't know how this *always* happens," he then said.

"Right," I said, "but I am in no way in love with you." Meanwhile, who the hell says gosh anymore?

"Okay," he said.

So many things can be misconstrued when communicating via text message. I took his "okay" as an: *Okay, sure you aren't, Mark. I can tell you totally love me.* When what he probably meant was: *Okay as in Roger that, talk to you later.* This is why we all need to just start picking up the goddamn phone and calling each other again.

I was so annoyed that Tom thought his shit didn't stink that I finally texted him back: "Dude, you're like my dad's age." Which isn't exactly true, but I think he got the memo that I wasn't interested in listening to how hot he thought he was because I never heard back from him.

My plan had backfired. I was not going to blog about every chapter of Alex Comfort's *Joy of Sex* after all, mainly because I was too lazy to try and find another guy to have sex with and I was planning on coming out of the summer STD-free, so there's my silver lining. I did, however, learn a very valuable lesson:

Whether they're eighteen or eighty-eight, all gay men are pigs and whores, myself included. I didn't really need a failed writing project to tell me that. I was not above sleeping my way to the top in order to get published, but luckily it didn't have to come to that. Instead, my first book came out from a wonderful publisher and it didn't even involve an AIDS scare.

THE P90X-FILES

Our beloved heroine has found himself with even more hurdles to jump. After beating alcoholism and getting his book published, Mark found himself still missing a certain something. In a stroke of brilliance, Mark decided to take a new approach to dating and working out while smoking an absurd amount of cigarettes that Lucille Ball herself would have been disgusted by. Everything in our heroine's life has led up to this one final effort in finding the perfect body.

This is the true story of one homosexual ... picked to live in Manhattan, work out every day and write about it, to find out what happens when Mark stops getting drunk and starts getting real ... annoyed. This is the P90X-Files.

Everyone always asks me, "Mark, how are you so fabulous? I mean, you've gotten sober, against all odds, now what? You have a published book, you look amazing, and you're a productive member of society. How can you have it all?" But what does "having it all" entail? A year and a half after I stopped drinking, I was finally beginning to feel like a normal human being again. I had a fabulous apartment on the Upper West Side with my lesbian life partner, a job I hated, but a job nonetheless, and a published book. I was happily sober and living as a functioning adult, but something was missing. For the first year of sobriety, I refrained from dating. I did not kiss, fondle, hold hands with, stick my dick in, or even cuddle another man. After hitting the big 3-6-5, I decided it was time to start putting myself out there again, and the results were nothing if not hilarious. For the first half of 2010, I went on date after date and quickly realized that while I had stopped drinking and calmed my life down, everyone else was as crazy as ever. After dating a Venezuelan who only had the word *pinkberry* in his English vocabulary, a buyer for a clothing line who went to China on business and never returned, an alcoholic who went to Las Vegas and never returned, several men named after major players in the Bible, and a lawyer who was dating so many men at the same time that he had to go to Daters Anonymous, I decided I needed to take a new approach to dating.

During the summer of 2010, I decided that it was also time to shake things up on the workout front. I had been doing the same routine for several years and I wanted to revamp my humdrum habits. My lesbian life partner (LLP) had started doing P90X, the home workout system, and was thrilled with his results. P90X is a twelve-week workout program designed to help people who are in decent shape get into great shape, and my LLP told me that this was exactly what I needed to get the perfect body I desired.

As the heat of the summer reached a fever pitch, I believed that a major change was upon me. Because after all, working out is like dating. No one wants to do it, but it's the only way to get to the end game we all desire: hot bodies and hot-bodied husbands.

To kick the season into high gear, I spirited away to Fire Island with Ron, my one and only Asian friend. He is quite possibly in the best shape anyone could imagine being in. He has cantaloupes where arm muscles should be and a washboard where his stomach should be. He would be the perfect male specimen if God had intended the perfect male specimen to be Asian. Ron was so good looking that whenever he was around, I felt even worse about myself. I met Ron a few years back through a friend in D.C. Ron was a financial adviser or something boring like that, but every time he tried to explain what he did for a living, I'd get bored and change the subject. The two of us met at Penn Station in our Unabomber attire (sunglasses, baseball caps, tank tops, and shorts) and began our rainbow tour of Long Island. Fire Island is a gay getaway off of Long Island that one must literally take two trains, a car, and a ferry to get to. We gays like to keep things as difficult as possible, or "exclusive," as we call it. Once Ron and I got on the train, the squawking commenced.

"Who are you fucking these days?" I asked Ron once we took our seats.

He laughed. Ron had just gotten out of a three-year relationship and was hell bent on sleeping with everyone he could get his hands on.

"Well, I am currently sleeping with an Israeli who is still at my apartment as we speak, an Australian dance teacher, and some white guy named John."

"Seems as though you have your own little United Colors of Benetton thing going on."

"Fuck off," Ron replied. "Who are you sleeping with?" Ron eyed at me as I looked down at the magazine I had brought with me. "WHAT?" Ron yelled. Suddenly, the gays on the rainbow tour ride to Fire Island all looked at us wondering what was going on.

"Shut up!" I said. "I haven't slept with anyone all year."

"Seriously?" Ron asked. "I am practically running a whore house on Tenth Avenue. How have you not slept with anyone at all this year?"

"I don't know. I just can't seem to find anyone I like."

"That's bullshit!" Ron said. All of the sudden he was very angry. Ron is a very emotional, very protective friend. He's the kind of friend who will start to cry if you approach him with good news or if something earth shattering has happened to you. He's also very in your face and to the point and knows when he's being lied to. "You're not trying, are you?"

"Well—"

"You're not!" Ron interrupted. "I can tell by the look in your eyes you're not. It's because of Dr. Jake, isn't it?"

"What?" I said, pretending I had forgotten about my most hated super ex-boyfriend. Dr. Jake was a married man I had dated right around the time I had decided to get sober. Because his life was such a mess, he seemed determined to undermine my efforts in getting sober. Needless to say, his machinations left me distrusting anyone with a penis and led to my dateless year and a half. "Of course not."

"You're lying to me. You still can't get over what he did to you. Listen, Mark," Ron said, "you are too fabulous to be single forever. You are going to have to at least try dating again."

"I dated all throughout the spring. They were a bunch of fucking losers, but I dated nonetheless. Besides," I said, abruptly changing the subject, "I don't seem to know how to find good men to date anyway."

Ron reached into his pocket and pulled out his iPhone. "Get one of these."

"I have a cell phone, Ron. It's 2010."

"You don't have an iPhone. You want to know how I manage to keep that rotating door on my apartment in full swing?" Ron tapped his phone and brought up a page that was filled with little pictures of men. "Grindr. It's an application on iPhones that allows you to 'meet' men by telling you where they are in relation to your current location using GPS."

I took Ron's phone out of his hand and looked at his Grindr. I looked at all of the pictures on it and quickly realized that everyone on his phone was also on the train. We literally *were* on the rainbow tour. I was practically the only person on the train who didn't have Grindr. Suddenly I felt like an outcast among my own people. It must be what Clay Aiken feels like on the daily.

"Just get an iPhone. It will change your life," Ron said.

"Thanks, but I don't think Grindr is where I am going to find my next boyfriend," I said.

"I currently have an Israeli in my apartment who would say otherwise."

"Whatever," I said. "I never thought you could contract an STD from your cell phone, but I guess I was wrong."

Ron began to laugh uproariously: "You are so fucking funny, Mark. It's a gift."

"Herpes is no gift."

Once Ron and I arrived on Fire Island, the real shit show

began. I've always said if you ever want to feel bad about your-self, go to a room filled with gay men. However, if you ever want to kill yourself, apparently you should go to Fire Island. Every-where Ron and I looked, there was one ripped man after the next. We kept yelling our mating call of "BODY BE RIGHT," which we say whenever we see a hot guy approach. We say it because I think we think we're black girls, and because we think it's endearing in some way, but it never works. Going to Fire Island and seeing all of these perfectly toned men made me realize even more that I needed P90X if I was going to roll with the big dogs this summer and find a husband. After twelve hours of only being flirted with by women in their midforties, Ron and I went back to the heat of the city. On my way home I made a quick pit stop because there was something I desper-ately needed if I were to move on with my summer successfully.

"One iPhone please!" I said.

"Your iPhone won't be ready for two weeks," the woman at the Apple store said.

"GODDAMN IT!" I yelled as I stormed out of the Apple store. There was one thing I didn't have to wait for.

Week One

After inadvertently being made to feel horrible about myself on Fire Island, I popped my first P90X DVD into my DVD player and was introduced to Tony Horton, the "ringleader" of P90X. Tony is about forty-five years old, built like a Greek god, and has a flapping mouth that just won't stop talking. At first sight, I was attracted to Tony, but much like every man I've been attracted to before, once he starting talking my infatuation quelled. Tony went on and on about how P90X was going to change my life if I stuck to it and how happy I was going to be with the results. I found this all very entertaining considering he didn't know me, my life, or what was going to make me happy. He kept talking and talking and talking until finally I realized that I had popped the "Welcome to P90X" DVD and not the actual workout into my DVD player. I realized this about thirty minutes into the welcome DVD. I decided it would be best if I smoked a cigarette, regrouped, and came back to the workout.

After smoking three cigarettes, eating a bag of Swedish fish, and chatting on Skype with my brother for a half hour, I came back to Tony, ready for a workout. The first workout in the program is chest and back. I began the DVD and quickly realized that the chest-and-back workout that Tony had planned for me was simply a series of pull-ups and push-ups, neither of which I was very good at. About halfway through the workout, I stopped to take a breath. After doing about two-hundred pull-ups and half as many push-ups, I began to think that Tony Horton was not actually trying to help me, but punish me for something horrible I had done in another life. I was in pretty good shape, but I had never been in such pain before. I took a break to smoke one more cigarette and gather my bearings. When I resumed the DVD, I was more than horrified to find out that the second half of the workout was just the first part of the workout in reverse. I shrugged my shoulders, bit the bullet, and got down to business. I hadn't come this far to give up now. I finished at a snail's pace only to find out that after the chest-and-back workout was over there was another fifteen-minute abdominal workout that followed. I figured since it was my first day and I had been tortured enough, I would throw in the towel for now and refocus for tomorrow. Besides, between the welcome DVD, multiple cigarette breaks, and girl talk with my brother, this had now become a two-and-a-half-hour ordeal and I needed to get to work.

I hopped into the shower after working out and began to lather, rinse, and repeat, but when it was time to wash my hair I could not lift my arms to reach my head. Suddenly, I was in more pain than I was after losing my V-Card. It took me about as long to shower that day as it did for Britney Spears to get her act together after that head-shaving fiasco. Once I had finally lifted my arms to wash my hair, I couldn't put them down. Always resourceful, I grabbed my left arm with my right arm and yanked it down, much like Dorothy had done with the Tin Man in *The Wizard of Oz*. I did the same with the other arm, got out of the shower, and dried myself off, then spent a full ten minutes putting on a T-shirt. If this was how I was going to feel after every workout, I wondered how long I was going to be able to continue with it, as it hurt to even put a coffee cup to my mouth that day.

I basically drugged myself to sleep and the next morning woke up still rusty but ready for day two of working out. The second P90X DVD is a plyometrics workout, which translates in normal-people talk to "jump-training," which translates to retard talk for people like me to "jumping up and down like a moron for an hour while trying not to knock yourself out." Already annoyed with the ramblings of Tony Horton, I muted the TV and tried to replace his voice with the musical stylings of Britney Spears. I realized quickly he was contorting his body in ways I had never seen a human being do before and reluctantly brought Tony back to life. After finishing the warm-up, he explained what jump-training was and I wanted no part of it. Plyometrics is a series of miniworkouts that focus on strengthening your glutes and legs. Each miniworkout was thirty seconds long, followed by three more miniworkouts, then a minute-long workout, and then the rotation was repeated.

"You can do anything for thirty seconds. Right?" Tony asked with his pearly white teeth gleaming on my TV screen.

"Fuck off," I said aloud. After our foray into the chest-and-back arena the day before, I trusted Tony even less than the "homeless" man on my corner who was always asking for a quarter but miraculously could afford a cell phone.

"Remember, folks, plyometrics is like swimming. Don't eat for an hour before working out," T-bone then said.

I had just eaten my usual breakfast of cheesy eggs and thought his disclaimer was a bit late. I always ate like crap at the beach before I went swimming and never drowned so I figured I would be cool doing this workout. As Tony continued blabbering on, he introduced me to the people who were working out with him. I liked to think of them as his backup dancers. They were there to create a nice effect, but never spoke or had any personality whatsoever. On the plyometrics DVD, Tony's backup dancers were the black girl, the Jewish guy, and Pete. Pete was there to make me feel horrible about myself because as we concluded the warm-up, it was revealed that Pete only had one leg, and the other was prosthetic.

"Jesus, you have to be kidding me," I said. I was already exhausted from the ten-minute warm-up and now I had this one-legged wonder judging me. The way he looked at me had the air of a cocky little son of a bitch. His eyes said, *"Look at me, I have one leg and even I'm in better shape than you are!"*

The warm-up concluded and the real workout began. I began following Tony and his team as they jumped up and down, squatting and lunging and crouching like the Jedi Knights they weren't cool enough to be. After the first series of workouts concluded, I realized I was sweating like a wildebeest. Beads of sweat were pouring down my face. I looked up at Tony and his friends as they were taking their thirty-second break. They looked fresh and ready for the next series of workouts. I looked at myself in the mirror in my room. I looked like I had just run a twenty-six-mile race where I was brutally gang-raped at the end. Before I knew it, it was time to resume working out. Tony was not fucking around during this whole jump-training fiasco. There were six more sets of workouts, each more excruciating than the next. As the plyometrics DVD came to an end, I suddenly realized why Tony had told me not to eat beforehand, because I'd never felt more nauseous before in my life. Pair that with the fact that I was sweating as much as Oprah and Gayle do when questioned about their sexuality. By the time the DVD concluded, I nearly passed out, I was so physically exhausted. I hopped into the shower and tried to stop sweating, but beads of sweat were pouring down my face. I showered for a full thirty minutes and when I wouldn't stop sweating, I decided it would be best if I simply dried myself off and walked around my apartment naked. After an hour of pacing my apartment, chain-smoking in my underwear and still sweating my balls off, I put on jean shorts and a tank top (or my "gay-famer" look, as I like to call it—put a pitchfork in my hand and we'd have had a horrible reality TV series on our hands) and walked out the door.

The summer of 2010 was the hottest on record in New York and I realized just how hot it was after I walked down the street and began perspiring even more than I was while working out. I got to my corner and was drenched in sweat so badly that I wondered why I had bothered showering in the first place.

When I got to the subway station, I realized that my tank top was literally soaked in sweat. Before getting on the subway, I took my shirt off, wrung it out, and stood on the sidewalk for a moment. As I stood there topless, at least twenty people walked by looking at me. In my mind, two days into a new workout, I was now looking like a Greek god and everyone was noticing. It wasn't until a toothless homeless woman told me to "put some fucking clothes on" that I realized I was making a scene.

For the next three mornings, I met with Tony and company and did a shoulders-and-arms workout, a kickboxing workout, and legs-and-back workout. After each one, I felt better than the time before. Apparently putting your body through excruciating pain every day can make you feel better in the long run.

That Saturday, I hunkered down for my last workout of the week before I could take a break from it all, the yoga workout. For whatever reason on the bottom of the screen, there is a timer on all P90X workouts to let you know how long you have been working out and how long you have left. The yoga workout was a cool ninety minutes long and before I even got started, I was bored. I find yoga very relaxing, that is, until Tony Horton starts blabbering on and on. I could not get in the right zone, so about twenty-five minutes into the yoga workout I simply stopped trying and decided to eat a Skor bar in lieu of working out. That was my one and only attempt at yoga.

Since Sunday was my day off from working out, I decided to focus my energy on taking Ron's advice. I suppose I was too fabulous to be single forever so I went on Manhunt to see if there was anyone worth going on a date with.

My profile on Manhunt is pretty basic, with my tagline being "I don't give a fuck!" because . . . I don't. It tells everyone what I look like and what I am looking for, which is: white guys under forty to hang out with. It also says that I have a "swimmer's build," although I haven't gone swimming in over a decade. Naturally, 90 percent of the people who reach out to me are men in their fifties who are either black, Asian, Latino, or all of the above. I guess gay people can't read. Anyway, as I fend off creepsters, I do a quick search to find hot guys who look like Abercrombie models to no avail. I usually end up settling for someone who looks like a Sears Catalog model, but a girl can dream, can't she? After signing on, I immediately got a few interesting e-mails.

IWANNABLOWU wrote, "Hey, cool guy over fifty, looking for younger to travel with. Will pay expenses."

How flattering that someone thought I was a hooker. I truly believe that is the highest honor one can bestow upon another human being so I replied:

"Thank you so much but I can't travel anytime soon, and in this economic climate I don't think you should be offering to pay for people you don't know to go on vacation with you, but thanks."

IWANNABLOWU responded, "That's cool. Come over now and I will pay you to blow me."

Inviting me on vacation made me feel like at least a high-class escort. Now I felt like a common streetwalker so I blocked him. I know writing is not a lucrative career, but I am not quite ready to enter Hookerville. Yet. I got another message.

Rimfan88: "You look like you have a nice ass."

I found this comment extremely interesting, considering the only picture I have on my profile is that of my face. I responded:

"You know, rimming is a really good way to get hepatitis."

I didn't hear back from Rimfan88, but shortly after I was

asked to pee on someone, and some black guy asked me if I wanted to take part in some sort of gang-banging in Harlem. I politely declined both invitations and moved forward. Then, a twenty-year-old asked me if I wanted to take his virginity. I really had to think about this, but again declined the invite because if he was anything like me he would need a Vicodin and some serious consoling afterward and I still had to deep-condition my hair that day. Taking someone's virginity is a very personal thing and not something I ever plan on doing again. All of this was very time-consuming, so I decided to get a move on and wait for my iPhone to arrive so I could get grinding. Clearly I was getting nowhere trying to find a boyfriend on Manhunt.

Week Two

It was time to begin my second rotation with Tony Horton and his crew of well-toned misfits. Since it was Monday, it was time for another go at the chest-and-back DVD.

After having done the chest-and-back workout once before and realizing that it was simply a series of pull-ups and push-ups for an hour, I mentally prepared myself for what was to come.

Just pretend you're in prison for one hour and have nothing better to do because the other inmates will kill you if they find out you watch One Life to Live, I thought. *Think of how this will pay off and how hot you will look the next time you go to Fire Island,* I repeated to myself. *If you finish this workout you can eat an extra bag of Reese's Pieces for dinner tonight and not feel bad about it.*

Meditating on these things over and over again not only helped me work out harder but also helped me get through the workout in one piece and without having to stop for a cigarette break. P90X was the hardest thing I had ever attempted to do physically, and considering I am that guy who will literally abandon anything if it's too hard, I needed to tell myself these things in order to continue. I was really invested in this P90X business and wanted to make it work. I kept chanting to myself and before I knew it, the workout was over and I came out of the ordeal feeling pretty good. That is until I remembered there was a fifteen-minute abdominal workout that I had forgotten about the previous week. I then continued to do the abs workout, almost vomiting the whole time but finishing relatively intact.

After I was done working out, I decided to check my Manhunt account before heading off to work. My iPhone still hadn't arrived but I was feeling better than ever about myself. I leaned over my computer to check my e-mail and sweat began to roll off of my face and onto the keys of my computer. It was so goddamn hot outside that I was expecting to look out my window and find a giraffe pop its head in. I was officially in darkest Africa.

I logged on to Manhunt and saw a very attractive guy named Ben had e-mailed me back. We had a few exchanges over the past few weeks and he asked me if I wanted to grab a bite. Something about the way Ben responded to my e-mails bothered me but I concluded that I needed to take Ron's advice and at least try to date. He couldn't have been that bad and I had no plans that weekend, so I agreed to meet Ben that Friday.

To look as good as possible for my date, I followed the P90X routine to the letter. For the next four days, I did the shoulders-and-arms workout, the legs-and-back workout, the kickboxing workout, and the dreaded plyometrics workout. And maybe because that one-legged bastard was secretly judging me the whole time, I worked out harder than I ever had before. I was starting to feel great and smoke more cigarettes than I thought was humanly possible. Something about Tony Horton and his chain gang of workout buddies made me want to pound cigs after I was through working out. I figured since I had basically just gone through hell, each cigarette that followed a workout was considered a "victory cigarette."

That Friday I met up with Ben. He had a shaved head, was about my height, and had a lovely set of pearly whites on him. I love a guy with a big, bright Colgate smile.

"I'm so happy we're meeting," Ben said as the waiter poured water into our glasses. "We've been chatting for so long, I guess it's about time, huh?"

We sat and ordered our meals and continued talking. All I wanted to do was go downtown on a burger and fries, but I ordered a salad instead. I had eaten nothing but granola bars, bananas, and cigarettes all week and couldn't ruin my diet now. Besides, I hate eating in front of dates. I always think people are still judging me while I eat. I will always be a fat kid at heart, no matter how skinny I become.

"So, what is it you do again?" I asked Ben.

"I'm unemployed right now, but I'm an actor," he said. "I already know what you do. You're an alcoholic, right?"

"Uh, yeah, but that's not my profession," I said. Fucking Google ruins every first date for me.

"Right. I mean, you write about alcoholism?"

"Among other things."

"That's cool."

"So, what are you doing with your spare time since you're not currently working?" I asked.

"Not much."

"Come again?"

"Nothing," Ben said again. "I go to yoga, hang out with friends. That about completes my day."

"Seriously?" I asked.

"Yeah. I don't do anything."

"So do you audition or . . . ?" I trailed off. How do you do nothing all day every day in New York?

I didn't know that was possible, there's almost *too much* to do in this city.

"Well, I have a job booked for December, so until then, I am pretty much just hanging out."

We sat there and did not chat very much during dinner. As we were eating all I could do was wish that I had ordered that burger instead of the salad I was eating. I was so fucking hungry. Not only that, Ben was so boring, I really didn't care if he thought I was a fat-ass for eating what I wanted. What a waste of a "first-date salad." As we ate, Ben just stared at me.

"You know what?" he said.

"What's that?" I was grasping at straws. Anything Ben said had to be more interesting than staring in silence.

"I sang the basketball song from *Promises, Promises* for my last audition," Ben said.

Perhaps staring at each other in silence was more interesting than what Ben had to say. I tried to pepper the conversation with my predictions on who I thought was going to win *So You Think You Can Dance* and we reveled in our mutual love of the movie *Boogie Nights*. I wondered what Ron was up to. He was probably off at some fabulous party filled with Asians that I wasn't cool enough to attend. I wondered what Tony Horton was up to. He was probably off in the Hollywood Hills doing bench presses and taking his pent-up rage from all of the steroids he did in the eighties out on some helpless girl with no self-esteem. Hell, I was wondering what the fucking Dalai Lama was up to at that point, and while we're at it Lorenzo Lamas as well. Ben was so boring that I literally sat there and planned out my meals for the next week, which included granola bars, bananas, cigarettes, and now eggs as well. I deduced that it was best if I at least threw one protein in there.

As we finished our meals, the waiter approached.

"Would either of you like—"

I cut him off. "JUST THE CHECK!" I yelled.

"Oh," Ben said. "Are you sure you don't want—"

I cut him off, "No, I have to get going."

I was going to fall asleep if I had to listen to any more of Ben's inane ramblings.

Ben and I said our good-byes and I went home and ate a king-size Kit Kat bar. I was sweating my balls off from the walk home from the subway and had worked up quite the appetite.

Week Three

I bulldozed into my third week of the P90X workout. By day fifteen, I was finally beginning to feel better about working out. It took some getting used to, but I was getting the hang of it. That Monday I did the chest-and-back exercises with the greatest of ease. Tuesday I did the shoulders-and-arms workout effortlessly, and on Wednesday I rocked out the legs-and-back workout. Thursday came and went with an amazing kickboxing workout and on Friday I had all but mastered the plyometrics DVD. Tony and I had gone from archenemies to best friends in less than three weeks. I was feeling great about my latest workout endeavor and looking better than ever.

Saturday afternoon I got a call from an unknown 212 number and picked up.

"Mr. Rosenberg?" the voice on the other end of the phone said.

Fuck! I thought, another bill collector.

"Perhaps. Who is this?"

"This is Kyle from the Apple store at Lincoln Center. I just wanted to let you know that your iPhone is here and ready for you to pick up today."

"OH THANK GOD!" I yelled. Thinking that Kyle probably thought I was a crazy moron (and he wasn't far off), I replied, "I'm sorry Kyle, I just thought you were a bill collector so I got worried." I chuckled but got no response. Those Apple employees are like trained robots: They don't have feelings; they just reprogram your computers and send you on your way. They're like a one-night stand. They give it to you good once and then you never hear from them again. "All righty, I will be by later to pick up my phone."

I didn't know if I was more excited that a boy was actually calling me or that my iPhone was finally ready, so after work, I ran to the Apple store to pick up my new best friend.

As soon as I had my iPhone in hand, I went straight back to my apartment and downloaded Grindr, created a profile quickly, and waited for every eligible bachelor on the Upper West Side to find me. While all of this was going down, Ron text-messaged me to remind me about brunch the following morning. I texted Ron back and told him that while I would meet him for brunch the following morning, he needed to communicate with me via Grindr or Internet Scrabble moving forward.

That night I started approximately 435 Grindr exchanges. I didn't need booze or even cigarettes anymore: Grindr was my new addiction. I was up all night, talking to strangers, planning dates, and virtually meeting every gay man within a five-mile radius of my apartment. I went to bed on a high.

Disheveled, I met up with Ron the next morning.

"Are you drinking again?" Ron asked as he greeted me.

"Of course not, why?" I asked as I sat down at our table.

"You look like shit."

"Why, thank you Ron, it's good to see you too," I replied, "but I'm not the one wearing a tank top with my nipple showing."

"I'm hot and I'm starving. Let's have a three-course brunch," Ron said. Body be right on Ron but girl loved to eat. That was one of my favorite things about being his friend. Every time we went out for a meal, we ate like champions. And not what you would think your typical Asian fare would be (rice, fish, etc.), but real American food like burgers, fries, and sundaes.

"How's the dating coming along?" Ron asked.

"Well, last week I went on a date with the most boring person I've ever met," I said. "And Grindr is a whole other story. That's why I look like shit. I was on the goddamn thing all night."

"It's addictive at first, but once you learn how to hone your cravings for it, you'll figure out it's the best thing that happened to gay men since the advent of water-based lube."

"What?"

"Never mind," he said. "It's too hot to be witty. Did you plan any dates?"

"That's the thing," I said. "I was talking to so many people that I honestly don't remember what I did."

"Girl, you need to keep your shit in check. But I'm proud of you for putting yourself out there."

"Thanks," I replied.

"BTW, body be looking right right now. How's P90X coming along?"

"It's going well. I still kind of hate Tony Horton, but I'm feeling better."

"I hated Tony Horton when I did P90X, but he's pretty hot. I'd fuck him."

"Seriously, Ron, who *wouldn't* you fuck at this point?"

"You!" he said as our food came.

After gorging on a three-course brunch with Ron, I made my way back to the Upper West Side. As I rounded my corner, a very well-toned Asian man in his late twenties stopped me.

"Mark?" he asked. "Is that you?"

Oh my God! A fan! I thought. Weeks earlier, I had run into a girl on the subway who had been such a huge fan of my book that she insisted I tell her any details of my life that weren't in it and take a picture with her. My fame had finally reached my own block. I was so excited.

"Yes," I said.

"Oh my God! Mark, I can't believe it's you!" the man said.

I brushed my hair to the side and wiped the sweat from my brow.

"It's me!" I said with a smile.

"Wow. You're so much cuter in person," the man said.

"Oh, I know!" I replied. "That picture on the back of the book does me no justice whatsoever."

"Uh—"

"Listen, if you live on this street, I would be more than

happy to walk back to your apartment and sign your copy of my book for you."

"Your book?" the man said.

"Yeah. My book."

"I'm sorry," the man replied, "I don't know what you're talking about."

"Oh." I sighed. "I thought you had read my book or my epic blog."

"I didn't know you wrote a book," the man said. "We spoke on Grindr last night. You told me we could have game night at your apartment this week."

Seriously? I thought. *I agreed to a game night? On Grindr? WTF?*

"You said you were going to invite your friend Ron over for a night of Celebrity at your place."

"Ron?" I said. What the hell was I thinking last night in my delirious state of grinding? Did I have delusions of starting a Pan-Asian alliance on the Upper West Side?

"Oh," I said. I felt like such an asshole. Here I was thinking this guy wanted my autograph when all he wanted to do was have some sort of Gaysian networking event at my apartment. "Yeah," I said, brushing it off, "maybe next weekend?"

"Sounds great," the man said as I began to walk away. "Oh, Mark?"

"Yes?" I said, turning around to face him again.

"You're way too skinny. You should eat something."

I turned around and floated home. I was elated. That was the first time another gay man had told me I was skinny. P90X and my iPhone were paying for themselves.

Week Four

Just when I had come to love and trust Tony Horton, he switched things up on me. I knew it had to be too good to be true. I was finally getting the hang of the routine when suddenly everything was different.

Apparently, during week four of P90X, we are to take a break from lifting weights and focus on cardio and core workouts. The first workout during week four is a yoga workout. Having already decided that Tony and I were never going to be able to do yoga in the same room together, I thought it best if I went for a leisurely run outside. We were breezing into July, and it just seemed to be getting hotter, but I figured if I ran outside in the heat I would burn a few extra calories and not feel so bad about skipping over the yoga DVD.

In high school I ran track but was kicked off the track team when I got caught smoking cigarettes. Ten years later, I found myself running around Central Park in sub-Saharan temperatures for my own enjoyment. As I was making my way back home, I glanced in the rearview mirror of a car parked on my street and couldn't believe what I saw in the reflection. I was finally the athletic young man that my father had always hoped for. I was in the best shape I had ever been in, and although I was going to smoke a half a pack of cigarettes when I got home, I was a whole new me.

When I got home, I lit up a victory cigarette and checked Grindr. I was trying to take it easy because the previous week I had gotten so wrapped up in grinding that I had literally lost sleep over it. After a brief twenty-four-hour break, I was thrilled when I received a note from Isaac, an Israeli hottie who wanted a third for a three-way with his boyfriend. I had never been in a three-way before, although I had attempted one earlier in the year that didn't work out because they didn't want to ménage with a smoker. I had found that smoking had become a recent problem with daters. No one likes cigarettes anymore. For a country that was founded upon the production of tobacco, I find it a huge slap in the face to our Founding Fathers that no one appreciates smoking anymore. Whenever I would go out with nonsmokers I was constantly looked down upon for my patriotic habit. I would tell said friends that if I was not able to smoke while out with them that there was a good chance I would be forced to fall off the wagon at any moment. I needed to smoke, if for nothing else than the sake of my sobriety. Nevertheless, I found that the best way to tackle this problem was to lie and say I didn't smoke, shower before meeting my prospective date, then chain-smoke afterward.

Isaac asked me to come over to have a three-way with him and his boyfriend, Elijah, after work and I accepted. I was twenty-seven and possibly the only gay person I knew who had never been involved in a ménage à trois, and since they lived close, I could put as little effort into it as possible. I put Britney Spears on my iPhone and listened to "3" the whole way there, in order to pump up for the big event. She has an appropriate song for everything, doesn't she?

I went to the Israeli's apartment and checked in for my three-way on Foursquare. I was greeted by Isaac, who introduced himself and Elijah.

"Sit," Isaac said.

"So how are things in Israel these days?" I asked like an idiot. I would like to point out that in adulthood, there is nothing I love more than hot Israelis. I love them almost as much as

I used to love sucking the grease out of chicken nuggets before they made them all white meat.

"Uh, we don't know. We've lived here for like five years... but probably not good, come to think of it," Elijah said, with absolutely no trace of an accent.

"Awesome, I am Jewish," I said.

"Aksfhksdufhsdjfgm," Isaac said in Hebrew.

"Ha-ha-ha, I have no idea what the fuck you just said," I said. "I am Jewish in name only, really. The only thing I can say in Hebrew is, 'We don't have tickets for *Jersey Boys*.'" I laughed as if it was the funniest thing I had ever said, but both gay Jews looked confused. "It's a long story..."

"Shall we?" Isaac asked as he gestured toward the bedroom.

These Israelis really needed to work on their hospitality. I wasn't even offered coffee or cake—we were apparently just going right for it.

The three of us went into the bedroom. Isaac was really hot and Elijah was pretty hot and they both spoke English, so things were looking up. We all made out. Isaac was really into me so he was paying more attention to yours truly, but Elijah didn't seem that into it.

"Akasjfhlasd?" Isaac asked Elijah in Hebrew.

Damn it! Why had I not gone to Hebrew school like a good little Jew? My ex-stepmother's machinations when I was a child were now coming back to bite me in the ass. If I didn't hook up with the hot Jews, this could be something else I could blame Stacey for.

"Akfdjhasdkfgjh," Isaac said in return.

"Is everything okay?" I asked.

"Yes," Isaac said as he continued kissing me.

"I am just not that into this," Elijah said.

"Then you can watch," I said. "It's fucking hot outside and I came all this way." I really hadn't come that far, but was feeling lazy and horny, so I had to make it as much about me as possible.

Isaac was really into me and was the hotter one, so when he kept kissing me and Elijah patiently watched, I thought, *Okay, so maybe I am not going to have a three-way, but I could potentially get some from a hot Israeli.*

"You have to go," Elijah finally said.

"What?" I asked.

"We cannot do this."

"Seriously?" I said. "But I am supposed to be the special guest star. You know, the one who comes in to spice up your relationship."

"Excuse me?" Elijah asked.

"I am the special guest star. Like Heather Locklear on *Melrose Place*," I said.

They both looked confused.

After trying to explain what *Melrose Place* was, they both decided that a three-way was a bad idea after all.

I walked out of their apartment and immediately began looking for some sort of watering hole. I was dehydrated from my trip to Israel but decided to walk back to my apartment because I hadn't smoked a cigarette in a full hour and would most certainly need to chain-smoke on my way home. I was a little pissed that even with my new P90X body and the fact that I had pretended to be a nonsmoker, I still couldn't get laid.

I checked my Grindr one last time that day and had two messages. One was from Ron, telling me I was an asshole for not calling him back the other night, and the other was from a very cute boy named Blake. I was way too hot and aggravated to respond to either so I put my iPod in and listened to "From the Bottom of My Broken Heart" on repeat. God bless you, Britney Spears.

I refrained from working out for the rest of the week or grinding. Neither were bringing me any joy and I was beginning to feel sick from being hot all the time. That Sunday, I met Ron for our usual brunch.

"What the hell is wrong with you?" Ron said as I sat at the table.

"Nothing. Why?" I asked.

"You look like hell," Ron said.

"If you keep greeting me like that, I'm not meeting you for brunch anymore. Do you just hang out with me to feel better about yourself?" I asked.

Ron laughed. "Of course not. When I say you look like shit I mean you look like you haven't slept, eaten, or worked out all week."

"Uh, well that's better, I guess . . . I've eaten, that's for sure. I just haven't been feeling well."

"Have you been working out?"

"No, my arm has been hurting lately."

"If it's tingling you're probably having a heart attack from all the goddamn cigarettes you've been smoking all summer long," Ron said.

"Jesus, Ron! Don't you have anything to take the edge off of life?"

"Sex," Ron deadpanned.

"Right," I said as I put my face in my menu.

"Listen, Mark," Ron said as he took a sip from his iced coffee, "I know you're not feeling well now, but things will get better."

"Will they, Ron?" I asked. "Will they? Because right now I hate my life—I hate my job. I hate dating and I hate Tony Horton. How the fuck do you suppose things are going to get better?"

I was making a small scene. Everyone in the restaurant was now looking in our general direction.

"You need to relax," Ron said. "Take the rest of the day off and tomorrow, get back on the P90X and grinding. Try to make an effort. I know you're not feeling well, but that's no excuse to stop doing everything."

"You're right," I said. "I do feel like P90X is working, it's just a pain in the ass. As far as the dating goes—"

Ron interrupted me. "Listen, Mark, as far as the dating goes nothing. I fucked an Egyptian at my gym, a hot-ass Italian waiter who lived in Hell's Kitchen, and some white guy named Dante last week."

"Wow, Ron," I said, "you have your own little Epcot Center thing going on, don't you?"

"Shut up!" he said. "You're too hot to not be having sex or dating, so please do something about it!"

"Sure, I'll do something about it as long as we get dessert after brunch."

"Donut ice cream sundaes?"

"Perfect!" I said. "Jeez, Ron, you're like my relationship Buddha. Except, while still Asian, you have a much better body and a much filthier mouth."

I left the restaurant that afternoon feeling a little better. I decided that the next day I would get back on the horse and try harder to look better and date better.

Weeks Five, Six, and Seven

I decided that I would go ahead and skip the cardio and core week because I had sweated so much that I figured that getting rid of that much perspiration in one week was just as good as actually working out. The walk back from the Israeli's apartment alone was at least a half a P90X workout.

It seemed as though the majority of July would be spent doing a new series of workouts that Tony had planned for me.

The first was the chest, triceps, and shoulders workout. It seemed pretty basic, but Tony had a new crop of fresh-faced backup dancers, one of whom looked like my stepmother, Stacey. She was super skinny, had a huge head like Stacey, and looked about sixty years old. Apparently in every workout Tony felt the need to include someone with that "if I can do it, you can do it" attitude. Stacey's doppelganger and one-legged Pete did just that. The whole time I did the chest, triceps, and shoulders workout I found myself trying to one-up the Stacey lookalike, which just led to me being more sore and more irritable.

That night I decided to check my Grindr again. I saw that I still had a message from that cute boy Blake.

"Hello, my name is Blake," the message read.

"Yum. Rhymes with cake!" I replied. You can take the boy out of the fat camp but you can't take the fat camp out of the boy.

We got to talking on Grindr and before I knew it, we had exchanged telephone numbers, Facebook profiles, and e-mails. I was giving up all of my personal information to this kid. But what was not to like? He was a twenty-three-year-old actor, six three, half Mexican, had a tattoo, and was gorgeous. I never date men younger than me, men who are half Mexican, actors, or anyone with tattoos (you can't be buried in a Jewish cemetery with a tattoo and I always like to think ahead), but considering nothing this summer seemed to be working out, and I was determined to find love, I figured I could give this kid a try.

I invited Blake over to dinner the following night. I told him that I was going to make my world-famous fajitas. Not only were they world famous, but I felt fajitas would make Blake feel more at home because a touch of Mexican flavor never killed anyone.

"Can I bring anything?" he asked over the phone.

"Nope. I think I'm all set," I replied.

"My mother told me never to show up to someone's house empty-handed," he said.

"Your momma taught you right. How about dessert?"

"What did you have in mind?"

"Ice cream? It's hot as balls outside."

"Any particular flavor?" he asked.

"Anything but strawberry. If I'm going to eat the calories, I don't want to have them be fruit related."

"You're so cute."

Duh.

Blake came over that night and when I answered the door, it was as if someone had smacked me upside the head with a bag of bricks and was about to trade me into white slavery. I was floored: This was what Ron was telling me about. I felt an immediate attraction to Blake. This kid was special, but I didn't understand why. I was immediately enamored. This couldn't possibly be love at first sight. That doesn't happen in real life, that's best left to Hollywood and people who have the talent to convey such emotions on the silver screen–like Sandra Bullock. All joking aside, I was immediately invested.

We ate and got to know each other. At this point in my life, I feel like I need to send potential boyfriends a copy of my first book in the mail and have them read it before an actual meeting. It saves so much time for one thing, and for another thing it gives potential beaus a 240-page book that lays out all of the horrible things I have been through in my past and never want to revisit. I gave Blake the CliffsNotes version of the book and we laughed. As we continued getting to know each other, Blake mentioned that we had mutual friends on Facebook, one of whom was an old friend of mine named Jerome who used to perform in shows with my old roommate Sally.

"I love Jerome. He's such a little shit-show. We had some great times together back in the day," I told Blake. "How do you know him?"

"We don't actually know each other," Blake said. "We had, like, thirty mutual friends and finally someone told me to add him. We chat all of the time, but we've never met in person."

"I'm sure when you do end up meeting him, you'll adore him. He's wonderful."

"Well, he's doing a show out of town so I'm not sure when I will actually be able to meet him."

"That's a shame," I said, pretending to give a shit.

Blake and I continued chatting and he mentioned that he used to be a fat kid.

"OH MY GOD!" I yelled. "I was a fat kid! My dad even sent me to fat camp!"

He looked surprised. "Seriously? Because for a while there I was clocking in at around three hundred pounds."

"That's amazing," I said, "but you definitely don't look it now."

"Thanks, neither do you."

"You look like a . . ." I trailed off.

"What?" he smiled.

"I can't tell you."

"Say it!"

"Well, my friend Ron and I have this saying when we see a guy with a hot body. We yell, 'BODY BE RIGHT!' It's stupid, it's like our gay mating call."

"You're an idiot," Blake said.

"Better you figure that out now than three months from now," I said as I looked at him again. "But it's true. Body be right!"

"Since you're a writer, do you think you will write about me?" Blake asked.

"I have the same policy regarding writing about boys that Taylor Swift does. Don't do anything stupid, and I won't write about you. It's a disclaimer I give to everyone and just one of the many wonderful qualities Taylor and I share besides being gorgeous blondes," I said. Having mentioned that, I'm sure we can all see where this is heading.

Before I knew it, Blake and I were making out. Before I knew it, Blake and I were in my bed together.

"What about Jerome?" he asked.

"Uh, do you see him here right now?" I said.

"No," Blake said, "but I meant to tell you. We're kind of dating."

I rolled over and replied: "I thought you said that you hadn't even met him yet."

"We haven't, but we've been speaking a lot and I really like him. I told him that I wouldn't do anything with anyone else until we met."

"That doesn't make any sense at all," I said as I suddenly realized why I had never dated anyone younger than me. "Jerome isn't here. I am and we're in bed together."

"I know," Blake continued, "but I really like him. We're kind of dating."

"Sweetie," I said. I looked into Blake's eyes and saw so many red flags that I thought I had been transported back in time to Communist Russia. "I understand that you really like him, but you're basically pen pals at this stage. First of all, you cannot date someone you've never met. The word *dating* (an action verb) originates from the word *date*, which means physically being in the same room as someone and sharing any of the following: a meal, a drink, or conversation. You two have done none of the above, therefore you couldn't possibly be dating."

I didn't realize that the word *dating* had to be explained to a twenty-three-year-old. Moral of the story is, Blake and I had sex all night and into the next morning. It was the best sex I had ever had. I was sober, and was with someone who liked me, and it was amazing. I cooked him breakfast the next morning and sent him on his way. He was off to Las Vegas to see his family for a week. I knew I would miss him.

The next week of working out with Tony was like a dream. When you're working out to make yourself feel better, it's one thing, but when you're working out because the potential to have sex is in sight, it pushes you even harder. As I waited for Blake to return, I literally raped the next week of P90X DVDs. Tony and his cohorts had no idea what hit them.

Blake called a few days later from Las Vegas and told me he was returning the next day. I told him that in lieu of taking the subway in the middle of the night, I would pay for him to take a cab to my place and he could either stay with me or take the subway home from my place. He was a struggling actor, and I felt I should help him. Plus I really wanted to see him. Apparently, I was channeling Daddy Warbucks and smoking cigarettes lit with hundred-dollar bills that night, because I never offer to pay for anyone to do anything. Ever. Blake protested that he did not need me to pay for him to get home, but when he got off the plane the next night at one in the morning, he was singing a different tune.

"Are you sure you don't mind?" he asked over the phone. "I would never ask, but it's so late and the subway is going to take forever."

"Of course not, I offered," I replied, "but hurry it's late." Now, in sobriety, I go to bed every night at a healthy 10:30. I truly am the middle-aged woman I always wanted to be.

"Okay, but I just need to let you know I got a little hammered on the flight back," Blake said.

I suddenly realized why his desire to take the subway home in the middle of the night had disappeared—he was smashed. As I waited for Blake to arrive, I kept receiving text messages from him that read: "I can't wait to see you"; "I can't wait to kiss you"; and finally, "You're going to get some good loving tonight." I was so excited that someone was finally interested in me and I was returning that interest. I had tried for the last eighteen months to put the wreckage of all of my past relationships behind me. Suddenly I was beginning to think that I could date someone and possibly be in love without being wasted drunk.

When Blake arrived at my apartment he greeted me with gin-perfumed hugs and we chatted for a bit.

"How was Vegas?" I asked.

"It was wonderful. I got to see my family and play with my nephew. But I'm glad to be back. It was so hot there," Blake replied.

"Well," I said, "it's a cool one hundred degrees here, so welcome back." Blake kissed me and I felt relieved he was back. In the spirit of changing things up, I decided I was going to be upfront with Blake, lay my cards on the table, and be honest about how I was feeling. "I missed you," I said. "I don't know why, but I was kind of sad you weren't around." I paused. "Even though we've only met once and you were only gone for a week."

"I missed you too," he replied. We kissed again.

Then, old Mark came roaring back like a bat out of hell. I was curious about what was going on with Jerome so I questioned: "Have you been speaking with Jerome?" I had thought that since things seemed to be going so well between the two of us, perhaps he had phased out Jerome in the past week.

"Yes," Blake said. "I'm actually going to visit him this week."

Hold up. Wait a minute. Had I not just paid for his sixty-dollar cab ride back from La Guardia?

"What?" I said.

"Yeah, I am going to visit Jerome this week. We've been speaking for so long, I figured it was finally time to meet the kid."

"I'm confused," I said. "If you couldn't afford to take a cab back from the airport, how can you afford to go and visit Jerome?"

"Ummmm . . ." Blake trailed off. "I paid for the trip before I went to Vegas. Besides, you offered to pay for my cab."

"I understand that, I just wasn't expecting you to stroll in here and tell me you were going to meet Jerome this week. I had figured since things were going so well between the two of us—"

Blake interrupted. "I just need to do this. We've been speaking for so long. I feel like I at least owe him this."

That's the thing with kids these days. Gay guys in their early twenties think that the grass is always greener on the other side. That is, until they figure out what I learned long ago. It's not greener. It's actually not even grass—it's Astroturf. Blake and I went to bed shortly after that but I could not sleep. For one reason or another, Blake really affected me, and something about this entire situation did not seem right.

The next morning, I sent Blake on his way, but before I left him, I had to throw in my two cents once more.

"Please, for the love of God, figure your shit out," I told him. "I really like you. Please."

"I have my shit figured out," Blake replied.

"Whatever," I said as I got on the subway.

I went to work that day in a huff. I was probably huffing because it was a) a hundred-plus degrees outside, b) Blake was totally playing me and I was allowing him to do it, and c) I had smoked about sixteen cigarettes and it wasn't even the start of business yet. I had no idea what had gotten into me. Perhaps it was the intense working out or the heat, but I had such strong feelings for Blake, yet I knew it wasn't going to work out, so I did the only thing that made sense.

"Blake," I said into the phone later that day. "I'm sorry but I can't date you anymore!"

I was devastated that I had to dump Blake, because my feelings were so strong for him, but I knew it was for the best in the long run. I had thought I had fallen in love with him at first sight, but maybe not. After putting the phone down, I realized that I hadn't worked out yet that day. I popped in the back-and-biceps DVD and began watching it. Immobile.

I stared at Tony as he lifted his weights. He seemed so happy with himself and his physique that he must have been married for years. I did a quick Google search but found nothing about whether or not Tony was in a long-term relationship. As I continued watching the workout DVD and not working out, I began to wonder why it had been so long since I had been in a long-term relationship. I started to think back on all of the train wrecks that I had called relationships in the past and wondered why I even bothered dating in the first place. Before I knew it, I was not only not working out while watching P90X, I was eating a pint of Ben & Jerry's and sobbing into it. How had I come to this? I text-messaged Ron and told him that we needed to have an emergency meeting of the Babysitter's Club the next morning.

I met him at our usual place and sat down.

"Aren't you going to tell me that I look like crap?" I asked.

"You yelled at me last time I said anything."

"Well, I've been crying all night and you know I am not a crier. Ice runs through these veins."

"I know," Ron said with a frown. "What happened?"

I filled him in on everything that had happened over the last few weeks.

"You love him!" Ron said.

"How was that the only thing you absorbed from my story?" I asked.

"I've never heard you speak about someone like that before. You must love him."

"Love?" I said, not fully understanding the meaning of the

word. "I don't think so. Besides, he's dating like half of America right now, I didn't know what to do, so I told him I didn't want to see him anymore."

"Why on earth would you do that?" Ron asked. "He's never met this other kid so they can't technically be dating. How old did you say he was anyway? Twelve? I mean, I had a pen pal once, but I never went to Tel Aviv to visit Shlomo, nor did I ever develop romantic feelings for him—because I never met him!"

"You had a pen pal named Shlomo?" I asked.

"Long story," Ron replied. "Listen, if you want Blake and I know you do, then fight for what you want. You tend to get rid of people at the first sign that something is going to go wrong. I understand that you're trying to protect yourself from getting hurt again, but if you like him, call him."

"I guess you're right," I replied. "Thanks. What's going on with you?"

"Nothing," Ron said. "I think that Israeli that I slept with last month is living with me."

"You *think* he's living with you?"

"Well, he hasn't left in almost a week. I don't think he has anywhere to go."

"Hmmm . . . that's peculiar. BTW, how were you able to meet for brunch on a Tuesday? Was it Asian Appreciation Day in your office? Did they give you the day off?"

"Fuck you," Ron said. "You're paying for lunch."

That night I called Blake and told him I wanted him back, but after a few days of going back and forth, we decided it would be best if we just stayed friends.

I stayed away from Grindr for the rest of July. It had bitten me in the ass so many times at this point that I figured I needed to lay off. I continued working out like a madman, however. I figured in the unlikely instance that I would run into Blake, I needed to look as hot as possible.

Week Eight

It was August, and although it was still hot, the heat was a bit more bearable. I was still reeling from what happened with Blake, but I continued as if I was all right. The truth was, I was anything but all right, and Blake and I went from "trying to be friends" to just communicating via virtual Scrabble. Turns out, Blake was quite the savant when it came to Scrabble. He beat my ass repeatedly and I quickly found out that words like *dick,* *June,* and *DOOL* (an acronym for *Days of Our Lives*) are not acceptable Scrabble words. I also found out that I had forgotten how to communicate with other human beings normally. I now only spoke with people through Grindr or Scrabble. I was officially a product of the Apple Company.

It was time for another week of cardio with Tony and the gang. I popped in the kickboxing DVD and realized that I could mouth the words that Tony was going to say before he said them. As with every other relationship I had ever had, Tony Horton was becoming a pain in my ass. Everything he said was beginning to annoy me, especially his comments about making soup. In an effort to be funny and lighten the mood after working out, Tony would always refer to an after-workout stretch as "stirring a pot of soup" and would ask his workout buddies what kind of soup they were making.

"Tomato soup," the blond slutty-looking one would say.

"I'm making lobster bisque, Tony!" the Jewish-looking one would say.

"Sounds like a lot of calories," Tony would respond.

"ACTUALLY, IT SOUNDS FUCKING AMAZING," I would yell at the TV.

"I'm making chicken barley soup," the Asian hottie would say. "What kind of soup are you making, Tony?"

"German po-ta-to soup!" Tony would bark in a horrible German accent.

"FUCK OFF!" I'd yell.

That weekend, Ron called me and told me that he was in L.A. and would not be able to meet for our usual brunch. I asked him if there was some sort of Asian convention going on and he told me to fuck off.

Weeks Nine and Ten

I hadn't heard much from Blake, Ron, or anyone else in more than a week, so I decided to give Grindr one final try. I couldn't possibly become a twenty-seven-year-old recluse, so I scheduled two dates with two lovely-looking Jewish boys on the same night. If neither date worked out, at least I would be one step closer to living out my lifelong dream of opening up a Hillel on the Upper West Side.

The first Jew I went out with was Andy. He was a bit younger than me, a bit shorter than me, and a bit hairier than me. While speaking on Grindr, he was constantly asking me if I wanted a blow job, and after I politely declined five times, he agreed to meet for coffee at a café near my apartment. I have the same policy as Kelly Clarkson as far as hooking up goes: I don't do it. Except for that pesky time with Blake.

Andy entered the café and greeted me with a kiss on the cheek.

"It's so nice to meet you," Andy said as he sat down at my table.

"Nice to meet you too."

"So, where are you from?" Andy asked.

"Outside of D.C."

He nodded. I assume he accepted that as a reasonable answer.

"How long was your longest relationship?" he said.

"A year and a half."

"Good. I don't date anyone who has not been in a yearlong relationship at least."

I sighed. Another bullet dodged.

"Where did you go to school?" Andy asked.

"Uh, are you looking to fill some sort of position or for a boyfriend?"

He chuckled and quickly returned to the conversation.

"No. Seriously, where did you go to school?"

"I went to school here in the city."

"Average GPA?"

"Are you being serious right now?" I said.

He laughed. "No, that time I was kidding."

"Oh, good. I was hammered for most of college," I replied.

He laughed because he probably thought that I was kidding, but I wasn't. Andy was pretty cute and seemed funny, so I decided to dig a bit deeper into who this kid was.

"When did you come out of the closet?" I asked.

"Funny you should ask that," he said. "I officially came out of the closet about six months ago."

"How old did you say you were?"

"Twenty-five," he said. "When I told my parents I was gay six years ago, they made me go to this camp every weekend to basically beat the gay out of me."

"Excuse me," I said, trying to refrain from doing a spit-take.

"My parents are Hasidic and were not happy when I came out of the closet, so they sent me to this camp."

I honestly wish I could make this shit up.

Andy continued: "So for about six years, every weekend I would go to this camp in New Jersey where the counselors would ask us certain questions about our sexuality and why we *thought* we were gay. Then every night they would hold us until we went to sleep."

"You have to be kidding me," I replied.

"Nope," Andy said. "Is that not the gayest thing you've ever heard?"

"Yes, yes it is."

Andy and I continued talking, and as if he were trying to impress me, he listed off every person he knew who had been on a reality TV show. I'm not impressed unless the person you know on a reality TV show has the first name Jill and the last name Zarin. After about forty-five minutes, I sent Andy on his way and in walked Jonah, my next Jew. That's right, I had two dates with two different Jews at the same café.

If I kept this up, I would be more popular than the Zabar's bagel bar on a Sunday morning.

Jonah (who I decided I was going to call "Super Jew" because he had explained several times during our conversation how much he loved being Jewish) and I exchanged the usual pleasantries and I got right to the questions. After nearly losing my shit in front of Andy, I figured I would be a little more to the point and see what made Jonah tick.

"So what are you looking for in a mate?" I asked.

"I really want to get married," Jonah said.

I looked him in the eyes, and when I realized he wasn't joking I told him that I thought I had just gotten food poisoning and needed to leave. I had been playing in the proverbial relationship sandbox with the kids all summer. I couldn't imagine committing to a second date with anyone, let alone a marriage. I left Jonah at the café and went home.

Perhaps I was destined to spend the rest of my life with Tony Horton. The thought made me a little nauseous, so instead of doing a P90X workout the next day, I went for a run. The weather was pretty comfortable so halfway through the run I decided to take my shirt off and run topless the rest of the way home. When I rounded my corner, I glanced at my reflection in a car window. I stopped to look at myself and was surprised to see that I now had a six-pack. My own body be looking right and I about said as much aloud to myself. I couldn't believe that I wasn't even finished with P90X and I had already seen such drastic results. I went home and Googled Tony Horton's personal information to see if I could send him a muffin basket as a thank-you, but unfortunately it was unavailable.

The next day at brunch, Ron's tune had changed.

"Oh my God, Mark," Ron said as I sat down at our table, "you look amazing."

"Thanks, but I'm a fucking basket case," I said as I leaned over to kiss him. "It's nice to get complimented for a change, though. How's everything? How's the Israeli?"

"Well," Ron said, "he's still living in my apartment, but we're seeing other people."

"Wow. You guys have played out a whole year's worth of story lines on *All My Children* in less than two months."

"Yeah, he has nowhere to go, and I like having him around but let's face it, I wanted to taste the ice cream, not buy the fucking ice cream truck! I have a few dates planned for next week. He knows about all of them and is okay with it."

"I don't get you at all, Ron," I said.

"What about you?" Ron asked. "Who are you dating?"

"Well," I said, "I went on two disastrous dates last week with two Jews and came to the conclusion that I don't need to be dating at all anymore. It's just not working and I'd rather be alone."

"Well look at you," Ron said. "You're just like Renée Zellweger in *Down with Love* . . . except without the puffy face of course."

"Thanks."

"Do you think you are just swearing off men because you still have feelings for Blake?"

Of course that's why I was swearing off men, but I replied, "Of course not!"

"I know you're lying to me, but I'll let it slide because I know you have serious feelings for him. Have you heard from him?"

"He texted me last week to say he's going on tour with a show for the next ten months."

"Perfect!" Ron said. "He'll be gone and that way you'll be able to move on!"

"I hope so. Otherwise I am truly pathetic."

"I loved my ex-boyfriend," Ron said. "We were together for

three years and I still think about him every single day. But we can't be together so I chose to move on and try to be happy."

I understood what Ron was saying but needed a few more days of feeling bad that Blake and I would never be together. I nodded and listened to what Ron was saying, but I didn't process any of it.

"Blah, blah, blah, blah, blah, but your body be looking right these days, girl," Ron concluded.

"Let's get a brownie sundae!" I said.

"Done!"

Week Eleven

When I put in my P90X DVD, something in Tony's eyes told me that he knew that our time together was coming to an end. My body had almost completely changed, and I felt amazing on the outside. On the inside, I was as big a mess as ever. As summer was ending, I was surprised when the temperature spiked yet again. Just when we thought the excruciating heat had left us, Mother Nature decided otherwise and brought one more week of horrible heat our way. After coming in from a run that week, I threw up all over the place because I was so dehydrated. It was time for summer to end and to move on, but there was also some unfinished business to take care of.

After I vomited, Blake called me unexpectedly and told me he was coming over. I suspected he was hammered because he had said on the phone that he was out at a bar with some of his new cast members. I quickly got myself together as best I could and waited for him to railroad his way back into my life, but I questioned his motives.

"I had, like, four margaritas," Blake said upon entering.

"Seriously?" I asked. "Four margaritas and you're hammered? That's pathetic and that's coming from a recovering alcoholic."

"I'm not hammered, just a little tipsy," he replied.

"Whatever," I said.

We sat and chatted as if we were old friends and there was no bad blood between the two of us. One of the reasons I really liked Blake is because I saw a lot of myself in him. One of the reasons I really hated Blake is because I saw a lot of myself at the age of twenty-three in him. Twenty-three-year-old Mark and twenty-seven-year-old Mark are two completely different animals.

As we continued chatting, I had to ask, "What the hell happened to Jerome?"

I had never gotten the skinny on what actually went down between the two of them, and being the nosy piece of shit I am, I needed to know.

"I haven't heard from him in a few weeks," Blake replied. "I don't know what happened. He just stopped responding to my texts and phone calls."

"Maybe it has something to do with the fact that the two of you dated for, like, five months and never met. Did you ever think about that?"

Blake laughed, "Yeah, I know how you felt about that."

"It's pretty ridiculous," I said. "But I have to say, having someone pick a stranger over me is a new low, even for me. So thank you."

"He wasn't a stranger, we had just never met in person."

"Right," I said with a laugh, "so he was a stranger."

Blake smirked. I suspected he was pretty hammered, otherwise he had no excuse for randomly getting so serious. "Mark, I just want you to know that I really love you as a person." And to make sure I understood exactly what he was saying, he continued, "As a friend. You're an amazing person. You're so generous and like no one I've ever met before."

Truth. Still waiting on the rest of the single gay population of Manhattan to get on board with what Blake and I apparently already know as fact.

"How do you feel about me?" Blake asked.

"I don't really want to get into this," I replied. I was, meanwhile, wondering why Blake needed to act as my bridge over troubled water all of a sudden. Until now, he had been my troubled water. His sudden interest in my feelings was questionable. I have a hard time telling people how I really feel about them and wasn't in the mood to get into it. Besides, I'm more of a "talk-shit-behind-your-back-and-wait-until-you-read-it-in-a-blog" kind of a girl.

I figured since Blake was going to be dancing his way across America for the next ten months, and he kept pushing for me to answer the question he already knew the answer to, it didn't matter.

"How do you feel about me? Just tell me!" Blake said.

"I'm in love with you," I replied. Stupid! "I think I fell in love with you the second I met you. And I'm pretty sure I've thought about you every day since then."

I am not one to get sappy, but I almost started crying. I've never told anyone that I have loved them while sober, and considering I'm pretty sure the only person I've ever loved was my first boyfriend, Sebastian, ten fucking years ago and I was completely hammered at the time, this was a big power play on my part.

Moral of the story is: Blake and I ended up fucking like he was going off to war. Technically, I guess he kind of was going off to war in a way. Touring the country and doing eight to ten shows a week can be taxing on one's knees. While we were making love, Blake, sweating like O.J. in a lineup, kept saying things like, "God, we would be so good together."

"Shut up, Blake."

We finished having sex and Blake left. I texted Ron that we needed to have an emergency get-together and he responded that he had news to share with me as well.

Week Twelve

My final week of P90X and I was feeling better than ever. As with any relationship, I was muting Tony Horton at this point and just watching instead of listening as well. We had been together for three months and the sound of his voice was bothering the hell out of me. Instead, I listened to a constant stream of Kanye West, Eminem, T.I., and Barbra Streisand (or as I like to call it, "My Gangsta's Playlist") as I worked out. I was so confused about Blake coming over and my feelings for him that every emotion turned into anger, so listening to rap and Streisand helped me not go completely over the edge.

Later that day I met up with Ron for brunch. He had chosen outside seating, so naturally I was chain-smoking.

"Why are you smoking so much?" Ron said.

"I'm a mess," I replied.

"How is this different than any other day?"

"Fuck you," I said as I put my cigarette out.

"Is this because Blake came over and had sex with you the other day?"

"How did you know about that?" I asked.

"You wrote a blog about it, you fucking moron," Ron said.

"I didn't know anyone actually read that garbage. Anyway, yes, that is why I feel like crap."

"I know you love him, Mark, but it's just not going to work out. I'm sorry."

"I know, Ron," I replied. "I've just never felt like this before."

"I understand, but these feelings will go away," Ron said. "I'm proud of you, though."

"Why?"

"Because after two years of not drinking, you allowed yourself to get close to someone and move forward from everything that happened in the past. Even if you never see Blake again, you've grown up. You fell in love, you lost your love, you've done so much this year, and you've managed to do it all without drinking. And body be right! So there's your silver lining. Nothing can stop you now!"

"And we can build these dreams together. Standing tall forever. Because nothing's going to stop us now," I sang.

"I'm trying to be nice and you're such an asshole," Ron said.

"You know I love you," I said as I blew a kiss to him. "You said that you had something that you needed to tell me."

"Yes," Ron replied. "I'm leaving."

"Ummm . . . okay," I said in shock. "Where are you going?"

"I'm moving to L.A."

"When?"

"This week."

"ARE YOU KIDDING ME?" I yelled. "How is that possible?"

"I have to for work."

"They're doing this because you're Asian, aren't they? Do I need to speak to someone?"

Ron laughed: "No, of course not. It's just the nature of what I do." I still didn't have a clue what Ron did for a living, but pretended to understand, and he continued. "I always knew I was going to have to leave at some point."

"What about your apartment?"

"The Israeli is going to take over my lease for me."

"Well, that worked out nicely, didn't it?" I said.

"Yes. I've rigged my iPhone to get my Grindr to work for L.A. residents, so I've already set up, like, four dates for next week."

"You Asians are nothing if not efficient."

"Fuck off."

"Shall we get donut ice cream sundaes one last time?" I asked.

"Of course."

Ron and I gorged on one final brunch and I sent him on his way. I was sad to see my good friend go, but knew he would be back to visit soon, if for nothing other than a great Grindr date.

I made my way home and could finally feel a chill in the air—the seasons were changing at last and I had finally stopped sweating. As I continued walking down my street, I checked Grindr and saw that Blake was 592 miles away, so I assumed he had made it to his first tour stop in one piece. I told him I would try and keep in touch, but I knew the likelihood of that happening was not good. We were destined to drift apart while he was gone. With Ron also leaving, I felt a very important chapter in my life coming to a close. Both Blake and Ron helped me realize that I could put myself out there and fall in love again. I could make new friends, be they Asian or not, and make connections without drinking or actually leaving the house, for that matter. For that I will be forever thankful to the both of them.

When I got home, I reached for a P90X DVD but realized that since I had doubled up earlier in the week, I was finished with the workout system. My time with Tony had come to an end as well. I looked in the mirror and saw a different person from the one I had seen at the beginning of the summer. There was more definition in my arms and chest, and my stomach was finally flat.

I sat on my couch and lit a cigarette. It seemed that even though I had changed inside and out, I had come full circle and was back to where I had began my summer. At least now I had not only my Marlboro Lights, but a six-pack as well.

SEARCHING FOR
JACKIE COLLINS

After three months that involved a rigorous workout
program, getting his heart shattered into a million
pieces, and canoodling with an Asian, our heroine
found himself lonely. Well-toned, but very lonely. In
another stroke of genius, Mark decided he didn't need
a man to keep him company when he could get a dog.

After my mess of a summer, I still found myself longing for
the companionship of another. All my life I had wanted
to be a middle-aged woman and soon realized I was quickly
becoming one. Night after night I would come home, alone,
watch the daytime television I had recorded from earlier that
day, and proceed to eat my feelings for hours on end. I needed
to find a new outlet before I undid all of the hard work I had

put into having the perfect body. Since I couldn't seem to find a boyfriend in this godforsaken town, I decided it was time to get a dog, because at the end of the day, it's nice to have someone to come home to. Someone who is going to love you no matter what. I figured since I would eventually have to feed and walk the dog every day, it would have no choice but to love me back. The best part about the situation is, the dog can't talk back, unlike every fucking boy I've ever dated. This whole dog situation may be even better than having a boyfriend and my best idea ever. For months I had been searching the Humane Society's database for just the right dog until, finally, I found him: a Maltipoo that was missing an eye.

It was instant love. This poor thing had been hit by a car and left for dead with its eye hanging from his socket. Now I'm not really a firm believer in love at first sight, except for that pesky time with Blake, but you know what they say: "You don't believe in it until it happens to you." And apparently, it was about to happen again.

The next day, I literally ran to the Humane Society to pick up my new best friend.

Once I got there, I filled out a mountain of paperwork, and after about a half hour, a lovely shit show of a woman named Bonnie came to greet me. Bonnie was a shambles. Her hair was a mess, her outfit was a mess, and her nails were a mess. Because of that, we'd hit it off right away.

"I'm Bonnie," she said.

"I'm Mark," I replied.

"Damn," she said, "you are just about the most gorgeous man that has ever walked through those doors. Did you know that?"

Bonnie had my number then and there. I was buying whatever the fuck she was selling.

Bonnie sat me down and we chatted. I was pleased to find out that Bonnie had the filthiest mouth of anyone I had ever met. We sat in a room filled with dirty cats and I told her that I wanted the Maltipoo with one eye.

"I want Jackie Collins," I said. "You know, the one that was hit by the car."

"OH MY GOD! JACKIE COLLINS WAS HIT BY A CAR?" Bonnie yelled.

"Not Jackie Collins the author. Jackie Collins the dog—the white Maltipoo with one eye. I've decided I am going to call him Jackie Collins, after one of my many idols in life. Looking into that one eye, I saw something special."

"Oh." Bonnie breathed a sigh of relief. Heaven forbid a car had hit the real Jackie Collins. I'd be wearing black until she was nursed back to health. "That dog's name is Mischa."

"Yeah, I don't like that name," I replied.

"But Mischa is a boy. You can't name a boy dog Jackie Collins."

"He looks like a Jackie Collins to me, and I'm the one buying the goddamn thing."

"Whatever," she said. "You can't have Mis— I mean Jackie Collins. At least not that Jackie Collins."

"And why the fuck not?" I said.

"Because he was hit by a car, Mischa—I mean Jackie Collins—is very temperamental. He cannot live with other dogs and your roommate has two of them. He attacks other dogs. Besides, if your roommate has two dogs already, why would you want another one?"

"Because," I said, "I don't think my roommate's dogs like me. They're always peeing on my shoes and I think they're plotting my death. Perhaps they're planning a horrible Jet Ski 'accident,' but you can never be certain about these things."

"I don't know what the hell you are talking about, but there are plenty of other dogs that are just as ready for a new home," Bonnie said.

"I don't want any other dog. I want that one-eyed little monster." I continued. "You see, Bonnie, I'm blazing toward thirty at lightning speed, and the closest thing I've had to a relationship was a half-Mexican playboy who has since been shipped off to do dinner theater somewhere in the Ozarks. For the past six weeks, all I've done is sit on my ass and eat while watching daytime television. I need the companionship of another or ten years from now, Oprah will be doing some sort of special on me titled 'The Six-Hundred Pound Man Who Hasn't Left His Couch in a Decade.' I mean, ratings would explode, but I can't be that six-hundred-pound man, Bonnie, I just can't do it! And since no man will have me, I believe a one-eyed dog is the most logical next best thing to save me from my gluttony!"

"It's a no go," Bonnie replied. "If the other dogs you live with get hurt, there will be big trouble. Let me show you the other dogs."

"Do they have two eyes?" I asked.

"Yes," she replied.

"I don't want a dog with two eyes. I want that one-eyed dog."

"Why the fuck would you want a one-eyed dog?"

"Because," I said, "a one-eyed dog means business. A one-eyed dog reminds me of myself: a scrappy, misunderstood outcast."

"Jesus Christ, you're not getting that fucking one-eyed dog, so let's move on. You don't seem to understand, you will not be able to walk down the street without having him attack every dog that comes along."

"Well," I replied, "I attack every person that comes my way, so it would be a match made in heaven."

My new best friend Bonnie had forsaken me. I was determined to get that one-eyed little fucker. Bonnie got so annoyed by my constant ranting that she called over Bill, the dog psychiatrist, to come and console me.

"I wrote a book about this kind of thing," Bill said. He was cool, calm, and collected; i.e., the complete opposite of everything I am.

"I wrote a book," I said.

"Did Bernadette Peters do the foreword to your book? Because she wrote the foreword for mine," Bill said smartly.

"No," I replied. "She is, however, mentioned twice." That's how gay I am.

"Well, then, please let me continue," he said.

"Wait," I stopped him. "Do you think Bernadette Peters will meet us for lunch? Perhaps she could shed some light on the situation."

"No." He was not having any of it. He was all business and continued. "You simply cannot take this dog home. Mischa—"

I stopped him: "Who?"

He put his hands to his head. "Jackie Collins..." I smiled and he continued. "...cannot be around other dogs. He is socially inept. We cannot in good faith give Jackie Collins to someone who already owns a dog."

I didn't believe him. I forced Bonnie and Bill to bring me to Jackie Collins at once. I was furious. I wanted this dog immediately and would not stand for such insubordination.

"I have Mary Tyler Moore on speed dial," I said once we got to where they kept the dogs. "And Sarah McLachlan for that matter!"

"Shut up, Mark," Bonnie replied.

Bill got Jackie Collins and when he brought him out, he leaped into my arms and began licking my face.

"This dog seems fine to me," I said.

"Wait for it," Bonnie said as Bill went back to the kennel and brought out another, bigger dog. The second Jackie Collins saw the other dog, this ten-pound Multipoo leapt out of my lap and began mauling the other dog. I've never had children, obviously, but I became overjoyed watching this ten-pound little asshole take down this thirty-pound dog. It's what mothers must feel when their child takes his first steps. I was overwhelmed with pride. I loved this dog. Jackie Collins (the dog) was such a little bitch. Sweet as pie when all of the attention was on him, but take the focus off him for even a second and he turned into a complete asshole. Sounds like someone I know. When Jackie Collins was done putting the beat down on the bigger dog, Bill returned sans rape-victim dog.

"You see what I mean?"

"He's fantastic," I said as I pet Jackie Collins. "He's everything I've ever wanted in a dog. And more."

"You can't have him," Bonnie said. Under different circumstances, Bonnie and I likely would have become lifelong friends, as with every other middle-aged mess of a woman I had met, but right now she was pissing me off.

"So what do you suppose I do?" I asked.

"Get another fucking dog," Bonnie said. Class act, that lady.

"Mark," Bill said, "why don't we call you when we get a dog that we think will be a good fit for you?"

"All right," I said. "But if you call me and I come here to meet either a two-eyed dog or a dog with all four legs, saying I will be pissed is the understatement of the century."

I left the Humane Society feeling defeated. That little one-eyed asshole stole my heart that afternoon. According to the city of New York, I am not only not allowed to have a boyfriend, but I am also not allowed to have a one-eyed dog.

FAMILY AFFAIR

Sure, Mark is no Oprah, but who is? Oprah isn't even Oprah half the time. But his struggles with food are a lesson to us all. Feeling particularly blue after the loss of so many people (and a one-eyed dog) he cared about so much, our heroine decided to take a trip home to see the people who made him the fucked-up person he is today.

When I go home for the holidays these days, my trips are quick and dirty. Kind of like a drive-by shooting, but less violent. The family is usually privileged to see me for about twenty-four hours, nothing more, nothing less. This past Thanksgiving, I sashayed home to see my brothers and sisters and a few new members of the family.

"Look who decided to take time out of his busy schedule to see his family," my mother said as I entered her home. "You can write about us, but you can't pay us a visit?"

"Hello, Mother," I said as I kissed her on the cheek.

"I made food," she said. "It's in the kitchen. Everyone has eaten already so you can have the rest."

"Oh, thanks, Mom," I said. "Leave the scraps for the former fattie."

"Shut up and eat."

I served myself the steak dinner my mother had prepared earlier and sat at the dinner table to eat alone.

"Don't forget, you're cooking dinner for the whole family tomorrow night," my mother said.

One of my mother's favorite pastimes is talking about what your next meal will be while you're already eating. It's one of the qualities I love most about her.

"Yes, I know," I said. "I'm having lunch with Dad tomorrow, and then I'll head over to Jamie's to cook."

"Why are you having lunch with your father?"

"Because," I replied, "he's my father. And I haven't seen him since his wedding." For all who were wondering, my father got rid of the serpent he was married to when I was a child and remarried a lovely woman named Carol. This is his fourth marriage. At the wedding, a few months before Thanksgiving, I was asked to give the speech on behalf of his children. I told my father and Carol to do their best to make this marriage work because it was to be the final time I would ever attend a wedding of his. The man is flirting with Elizabeth Taylor territory. Meanwhile, in most states it's still not legal for my people to get married once, let alone four times. What a joke!

"Whatever," my mother said. Sometimes when I come home for holidays, I feel like my mother may as well pee on me. She's as territorial as a dog and gets pissed when I spend time with anyone other than her.

I finished my dinner and quickly went downtown on a bag of peanut butter M&M's. Since I would not be working out for the duration of my time home, I figured it was my duty to eat as much as humanly possible before returning to work. As I wiped the residue of M&M's off my face and sat down to watch television, a wave of pain came over me.

Suddenly I felt about as sick as I was when I found out that my father had sent me to fat camp. I darted to the bathroom, stuck my head in the toilet, and violently threw everything up that I had just eaten.

"WHAT THE FUCK IS GOING ON IN THERE?" my mother yelled. "You're so loud! Jesus!"

"I'm sorry," I said with my head in the toilet bowl. "I can't stop throwing up!"

"Well, could you keep it down?" she yelled. "I want to finish watching the rest of *Army Wives* before bed!" I left the bathroom, opened my mother's bedroom door, and peered into a dark room seeing nothing but the glowing light of the television.

"*Army Wives*?" I asked. "Seriously?"

"YEAH, SERIOUSLY! SHUT IT!" she yelled.

"I THINK YOU POISONED ME!" I shouted.

She laughed. "Poisoned you? Why on earth would I do that?"

I went back to the bathroom and threw up again. As I wiped the vomit from my mouth, I lifted my head up again and yelled, "YOU'RE DOING THIS SO I WON'T HAVE LUNCH WITH DAD TOMORROW!"

"What the fuck do I care who you have lunch with?"

"I DON'T KNOW," I cried. "Maybe you're doing this out of revenge. You've always wanted me to move home!"

"MOVE HOME?" my mother yelled. "Why the hell would I want you here?"

"I DON'T KNOW!" I cried. "I'm dying! Do you have any Pepto?"

"No," she barked. "Now quiet down, my show is almost over and I can't hear a damn thing."

I felt like I had thrown up everything I had ever eaten. Just when I thought I was done, it just kept coming up. After about an hour, I made my way back to the couch. My mother, God love her, had had a rough couple of months. A few weeks prior, she had suffered what everyone had thought was a heart attack. Turns out she was having horrible chest pains as a side effect to the Boniva she was taking for her osteoporosis. Needless to say, Sally Field's in-box was flooded with e-mails from me that month with the subject reading: "How on earth, Norma Rae, could you forsake my family like that?" With all of this drama going on it was no wonder that my mother's cooking was on a downward spiral. I couldn't hold it against her.

As I sat on the couch, the room began to spin and I saw my life flash before my eyes for about the tenth time in my twenty-seven years on this earth. I pictured my ill-fated attempt at blackface, meeting my former stepmother, a woman who would change my life forever, and my trip to fat camp. I reminisced about falling in and out of love with Blake, Tony Horton, and a dog named Jackie Collins. Then I briefly thought I saw Jesus. Turns out, it was my brother Kevin getting a glass of water—his hair was just out of control that night. I felt like I was clinging to life. Since my mother had attempted to kill me, I felt it was my duty to wake her up in the middle of the night and tell her as much.

"MOM!" I yelled as I entered her pitch-dark room.

"What the fuck?" she said with a start.

"You tried to kill me tonight. I don't appreciate that," I said seriously. I was standing there in the dark like some sort of pe-dophile.

"I don't know what you're talking about, but I am trying to sleep, so could you please quiet down," she said. "And if you're going to throw up, please do so in the kitchen sink. Your bowels are very loud tonight."

"THAT'S NOT FUNNY!" I yelled. "I'm dying and all you can do is make fun of me."

"OH MY GOD, MARK, GO TO BED! It's 3 A.M.!"

"I would go to bed, but I've been vomiting out of my mouth and ass for the last three hours, thanks to your cooking."

"Get out of my room!"

I sat on the couch and quickly text-messaged all of my friends from my deathbed.

"We all knew it would come to this," I wrote my friends. "My mother has tried to kill me. I will do my best to pull through, but if I don't make it, please be sure to carry on my legacy. Love, Mark."

Shortly after, I received a text from my friend Ron: "OMG, girl. I miss you so much. Come to L.A. to see me. The guys are hot, hot, hot!"

I immediately responded: "If I make it through the night, I'll make my way out there."

"Fuck off," Ron replied. "You text-messaged me that you were dying last month and here you are: still complaining. See you soon! Love you girl!"

It became quite clear that neither Ron nor the rest of my friends understood the severity of my condition. I curled up in a ball on the couch and slept briefly. I had the most wonderful dream that Susan Lucci, Jackie Collins, and I were all drinking sparkling cider at Jackie's Beverly Hills compound.

When I woke up, my mother's house was empty, thank God for that. I was a complete mess. My insides hurt so much I concluded that the pain that I was in would be similar if I had had a back-alley abortion the evening before. I got up, went to the bathroom, and looked in the mirror. The bags under my eyes had dropped down to my knees and my complexion resembled someone who had jaundice. My body, however, had never looked better, so in my haze of delirium, I decided to snap a few pictures of myself so I could update my Grindr profile. As I finished my makeshift photo shoot, I saw that I had seven unread messages on Twitter from my father.

KMoney88: "Mark, are we still going to lunch today?"

KMoney88: "Where do you want to go to lunch?"

KMoney88: "Did you even make it to D.C. OK?"

KMoney88: "I have to walk the dog, can you let me know where you'd like to eat lunch?"

KMoney88: "Mark?"

KMoney88: "I'm going to the store. Can you get back to me?"

KMoney88: "Sasklfjasf" (I think there was confusion with that last tweet on my father's end)

Why on earth was my father tweeting at me all morning? Ever since that man figured out how to "socially network," he's stopped using the phone altogether.

I picked up the phone and called my father.

"What the hell is wrong with you?" I asked when he answered.

"What?" he said.

"Why are you tweeting at me?"

"I was trying to get your attention."

"How about fucking calling me the next time?"

"Isn't this what you kids do these days in order to get in touch with each other?" my father said.

"First off, neither you nor I are 'kids' any longer. Second, I firmly believe that human communication is making a comeback."

"Whatever," he said. "Are we having lunch or not?"

"Negative, ghostwriter," I replied. "Mom tried to kill me last night, so I think I'm down for the count."

"Your mother tried to kill me once," my father said, as if sharing a fond memory. "Those were the days."

"Right," I replied. "I think I got food poisoning last night, so I'm going to stay in. I'll see you next time."

"All right. I'll see you around, I guess."

I hung up with my father, drank a gallon of ginger ale and a liter of Pepto, and began to feel better. As I read text messages from friends wondering if I had fallen off the wagon the evening before, I prepared for my next feast. That evening I was going to cook chicken Parmesan for my brothers, sisters, niece, four nephews, and mother. I had sent out a meeting request on Outlook weeks before to make sure that everyone was available. Getting together twelve people in my family is like rounding up a traveling freak show, but it's always worth it. As I thought about all of the trouble I had gone through for the meal, I tried not to dry-heave all over the place. I wondered why on earth everything in my life revolves around things going into or coming out of my mouth. My life has been spent planning meals, burning off the calories of those meals, and occasionally throwing up or getting thrown up on. Is this what life is all about?

That evening, my mother and I drove to my sister Jamie's house for dinner. The entire ride was spent with me shooting her dirty looks and her refusing to apologize for nearly killing me. Once we arrived, we were greeted by my sister's children. I was not completely on board with the names that she chose for them, so I refer to them as Shlomo, Chaka Khan, and Emmanuel Lewis. It's no wonder the only godchildren I have are two Yorkies who live in Midtown.

"UNCLE MARK!" Shlomo yelled as he greeted me with a hug. "How's New York?"

"I'm hustling," I replied.

"Hustling?" Shlomo said.

"Eh, you'll figure it out when you grow up."

"How's my little princess?" I asked Chaka Khan.

"UNCLE MARK!" she squealed.

Chaka jumped into my arms and wrapped her arms around my neck. I smothered her with kisses. Chaka then rejoined her brothers in the living room as they watched television.

"MARK!" Jamie barked from the kitchen, scaring the shit out of everyone. I am happy to report that my sister has quickly gone from spastic party girl to spastic mother of three. "Don't kiss Chaka if you're going to get her sick. Mom said you had a stomach bug last night. I cannot have a houseful of sick children." I could barely get through the door without my sister barking orders at me.

"Stomach bug?" I said as I shot my mother the fifteen

thousandth dirty look of the day. "Uh, no, Jamie, she tried to kill me last night."

"What?" she said.

"She gave me food poisoning."

"Your brother and his wild imagination," my mother said. "No one else got food poisoning but him."

"Really?" Jamie said. "Then you must have had a bug. I don't want you around the children if you're going to get everyone sick."

"Relax, Jamie," I replied. My sister, mother of the century, is a psycho when it comes to her children and their health. So psycho that if anyone even comes near any sort of nut, they are not to be allowed into her house for up to a month due to Chaka's horrible nut allergy. "I'm fine!"

"All right, but if the kids start getting sick, you're going to have to go home."

"It's great to see you too!" I said smartly as I breezed into the kitchen to prepare dinner. My sister and mother followed quickly and began squawking like two hens about everything that had happened in the twenty minutes that they had not spoken to each other that day. As I began breading the chicken, my sister chimed in once again.

"Can I do anything to help?" she asked.

"Yeah," I said, "keep the fuck out of my way."

Jamie grunted as she and my mother moved their squawk fest to the living room as the children danced around them. Shortly after, my other sister Kim and her girlfriend, Meghan, entered.

"Look what the lesbians dragged in," I called out.

"Way to call out the lesbians," my sister said. "Hey gay boy."

I greeted my sister and her girlfriend, whom I adore, with huge hugs.

"How's my favorite homo?" Meghan asked.

I blushed. "You say that to all the boys, don't you?"

"Just you, my dear."

Kim and Meghan joined Jamie and my mother in the living room.

"MARK!" Jamie yelled.

"WHAT?" I yelled back.

"If you're breading the chicken with eggs, don't touch anything. I don't want the kids getting salmonella!"

"Jesus Christ," I said under my breath. "Everything is fine in here."

The ladies continued chirping in the living room. Since leaving town, my sister Kim has officially become the Empress of Gay D.C. She and Meghan began a gay dating service in town and now they hold court everywhere they go. It's almost as if she were Hillary Clinton and her platform was an STD-infested gay bar above a bathhouse. As I continued cooking, my brothers Kevin and Tony and Tony's wife, Nikki, and their children entered. I didn't care for the names they gave their children (mainly because in private, while hammered, my sister-in-law told me she was inspired to name one of my nephews after a Duke rapist, but said "he hadn't been convicted of any crime at the time of the baby naming, so it was okay"), so I call them Shmewy and Gordy. It's no wonder I wasn't invited to either of their christenings. The kids gave me a hug and went off to play with the other children in the basement.

"Hi, Mark," Nikki said. I absolutely adore my brother's wife. She is a complete shit show. She's super tall with ridiculously curly blond hair and says whatever she wants to, making me believe that the two of us are actually related by blood. If I were ever going to perform in drag, I would model myself after her. Having a drag queen replica of yourself must be the highest form of flattery you could bestow upon any woman.

"Oh, Nik," I said as I hugged her, "I miss you guys."

"We miss you. How's everything going in New York?"

"You know me, just hustling," I said as Tony made his way to the living room with the ladies.

"OH, HI, BRO," I yelled at Tony.

"Oh, hey, Mark," Tony said, looking away from me.

"GREAT TO SEE YOU!" I yelled. Tony ignored me and sat on the couch next to Kim and put his arm around her neck as if about to choke her. Some things never change. Even in your late thirties.

I continued cooking dinner and chatted with Kevin. We reminisced about how funny it was to think that we were once our niece's and nephews' age and now we are the uncles and have a new generation of family members to mold, teach, and corrupt.

I finished cooking dinner and the children gathered around the table to eat. All of the adults, except me, sat on the living room floor and enjoyed the glorious chicken Parmesan I had prepared.

My stomach was still unsettled from the previous night, so I stood in the kitchen and watched as my niece and nephews ate and fooled around with one another. There were five of them, just as many children as my parents had. As I gazed at them in awe of how amazing each one of them is, I couldn't help but wonder what the future held for them. I first looked at Shmewy, my brother's oldest boy. He has a quiet charm about him but will randomly burst out in a fit of goofiness, just like his father, Tony. Sitting next to him was Chaka Kahn, the most beautiful little girl I've ever seen. She's a mirror image of her mother, Jamie, beautiful on the inside and outside with a heart as big as her mother's. I then glanced at Shlomo, who has always reminded me of his Aunt Kim. Energetic and full of life with a personality that fills any room he's in. Next to him was Gordy, whose personality is very reminiscent of my brother Kevin's when he was a child: rambunctious, vivacious, and all over the place. When he grows up, he's going to be the life of the party, just like Kevin. Finally, sitting all the way at the end of the table, was Emmanuel Lewis. The kid is a mini me. Give him a few years and he'll have the fashion sense and quick wit of his most beloved uncle.

I sat and watched the five children laugh and eat dinner, and it made me think about their futures and also made me wonder when the fuck I became so sentimental. I must be getting soft in my old age. Perhaps one of them will be a superstar athlete while one of them will become grossly overweight. Perhaps one of them will take to the theater while another may hit the bottle hard. Perhaps one of them will be the class clown while another will be a silent genius. All I can do is love them and hope that they learn from the mistakes that their parents, aunts, and uncles have made. But if they decide to take the same road that we have, I hope it's paved with glitter, because no matter what happens in life, at the end of the day, all we have is each other, regardless of how fucking crazy we all are: It always comes back to the family.

As I sat reflecting on my family, my mother approached me. "Penny for your thoughts?" she asked.

"I was just thinking about something a very wise woman

once said: 'Family is like baking a cake from scratch. It gets messy.'"

"That's beautiful," my mother said. "Where did you hear that?"

"Miss Ellie said it on an old episode of *Dallas* I just watched."

"Idiot!"

"You didn't mean to poison me, did you?" I asked.

"No," she said. "But I was half in the bag when I cooked so who the hell knows how long I actually left that steak out for."

As I was reflecting on the next generation of shit shows in my family with my mother, I got a tweet from my father that said, "Hope you're feeling better."

ACKNOWLEDGMENTS

I'd like to thank everyone at Crown Publishing as well as all of the investors in Blackouts Productions for making this book possible. Big thanks to Jacqueline for taking a huge risk on me. Thanks to Amanda, Mauro, Campbell, Tammy, and Jessica at Three Rivers Press. Big thanks to my mother, father, brothers, sisters, niece, and nephews for keeping me going and letting me write about your lives and being so amazing about everything else. I would seriously be nothing without your support. Kristin, thank you for helping me with the editing process. You're a talented lady and a great friend. Thanks to my "sisters": Eric, Ron, and Andrew for your constant support and love. Thanks to Tom and Mike, Evelyn, Katelyn, Sally, Katie, Meghan, Tim, Krystal, Adam, Lisa, Shawn, both Jason Cs, Lori, Erik, Kate, Jeffrey, Laura, Joanne, Willie, Candace, Cameron, and, of course, the entire Schwab family. Also, big shout-outs to all of the illegitimate children I've acquired along the way—what a great group of kids. Finally, I'd like to thank Jake. I always told you I would thank you in a book, and without seeing what a horrible person you really are, I would have never had the ammunition and drive I needed to finish this book.

ABOUT THE AUTHOR

MARK BRENNAN ROSENBERG is the author of *Blackouts and Breakdowns* and writes the blog *The Single Life of a Manhattan Homo*. He currently resides in New York City and is single—so if you know of anyone, let him know.

Visit him online at www.markbrennanrosenberg.com.